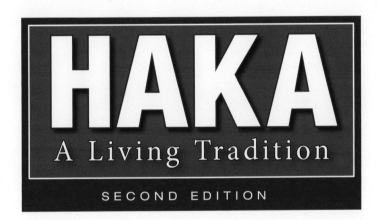

HAKA
A Living Tradition

SECOND EDITION

HAKA
A Living Tradition

SECOND EDITION

Wira Gardiner

Hodder Moa

To my 13-year-old daughter Rakaitemania and her younger sister Mihimaraea, who have both taken up kapa haka with a passion. And to my wife Hekia whose commitment ensures that the next generation is being well prepared to take kapa haka to the world!

National Library of New Zealand Cataloguing-in-Publication Data
Gardiner, Wira, 1943-
Haka : a living tradition / Wira Gardiner. 2nd ed.
Previous ed.: Hodder Moa Beckett, 2001.
Includes index.
ISBN 978-1-86971-116-0
1. Haka (Dance) 2. Chants, Maor . 3. Maori (New Zealand
people)—Social life and customs. [1. Haka. 2. Ngeri.] I. Title.
793.31993—dc 22

A Hodder Moa Book
Published in 2007 by Hachette Livre NZ Ltd
4 Whetu Place, Mairangi Bay
Auckland, New Zealand

Designed and produced by Hachette Livre NZ Ltd
Printed by SNP Leefung Printers Limited, China

Illustrations by Abel Viareta
Front cover photographs: Peter Bush (left) and Aaron Smale (right)
Back cover photograph: Alexander Turnbull Library

Contents

Acknowledgements

The author acknowledges and thanks Ainsley Gardiner for her research and her untiring efforts to bridge between her father and the Hodder Moa Beckett team; Lewis Moeau for his unfailing support and suggestions; and Belinda Ryan and Jon Collier from the NZ Army for their unhesitating help. Thanks also to the staff of the Alexander Turnbull Library, the NZ Rugby Union, the Aotearoa Traditional Māori Performing Arts Society and those individuals who gave us permission to reprint photos. Thanks to Kevin Chapman and Linda Cassells and the team at Hodder Moa Beckett whose confidence and persistence led to the first publication of this book in 2001.

In this update I want to further thank Kevin Chapman and his team at Hachette Livre: first, for their persistence in seeing the opportunity to expand the readership on the subject of haka; and second, for providing me with the opportunity to add further to this fascinating issue. To Jane Hingston, Managing Editior, a special thanks for mastering the art of gentle persuasion!

Finally, I want to acknowledge those around me who gave unstintingly of their advice and information.

Preface

This book is about the creation and development of an ancient dramatic dance form — the haka. Today the haka is an integral part of Māori and broader Aotearoa New Zealand cultures. When a stirring haka like 'Ka Mate!' is performed, most Aotearoa New Zealanders can mouth the words, keep the beat and thrill to the sight and sounds of something urgent and awesome. This short history of the haka is a journey of discovery, which takes us from its birth, through its development and application over the centuries to its emergence in the dawn of the twenty-first century as a national icon.

When Kevin Chapman, Managing Director of Hodder Moa Beckett (now Hachette Livre), raised the idea of my writing this book, I did a quick literature search and compiled a list of references related to haka. Remarkably, I found that there was an absolute dearth of contemporary material. When I asked specialists about aspects of the haka I got their personal views but could not find much supporting documentary evidence. I found this strange, given the importance of haka to Māori and its growing importance to the general public.

I was therefore delighted to accept the task as it gave me the opportunity to make the haka more readily available to the general public, to explain its history, to describe the various types of haka and the roles of men and women, and to review the role of haka as an instrument of nation building.

I thought it was especially important to deal with some contemporary issues surrounding its greater commercialisation as a consequence of the advent of professional rugby. In recent times there has been much controversy surrounding ownership of haka, especially the haka 'Ka Mate!', which raises issues of how or whether you can determine the intellectual property rights of cultural heritage. These and other equally important issues need to be raised and debated.

As we begin the new millennium we marvel at the growing influence of the haka on our lives. More national sports teams are engaging in the haka as a celebration of victory and as an expression of our unique identity, telling the world in no uncertain terms that we have something that no one else has.

The story of the haka begins with its origins in the mists of time, how it influenced the lives of our ancestors, the observations of it by the early explorers, missionaries and settlers and the way it has grown up with our nation as it matures. It is also about the way in which the relationships between Māori and non-Māori Aotearoa New Zealanders have grown through haka. It is truly a vehicle for enhancing our relationships, celebrating our differences and at the same time rejoicing in our successes.

In the six years since I first wrote *Haka: A Living Tradition* these views are no less true. Indeed the richness of the tapestry of the haka continues to grow as this updated version of my book will show.

Wira Gardiner
June 2007

Introduction: Personal reflections

Over the last few years the debate, the controversy, the intense emotional views around the haka continue to engage a wide spectrum of local and international attention. It is truly a reflection of the haka and its impact on the psyche of our nation and, for that matter, on the psyches of those who have to confront us on the sports fields across the globe. For those who are intensely curious about this wild and exotic dance from the bottom of the world there is also much to be observed and marvelled at!

When the publisher Hachette Livre NZ asked me to review my book, I jumped at the chance. For two reasons: first, because it provides an opportunity to expand on a number of the themes I began in my earlier book; and second, because it allows me the opportunity to expand the subject beyond the pure haka to include a number of other elements associated with the haka.

More and more New Zealanders are being exposed to and taking part in kapa haka. *Kapa* means to stand in a row. *Haka* means to dance. I think it is important to focus some attention on these associated elements, simply because they form with the haka a complementary set of entertainments. The haka on its own is powerful. Kapa haka brings a multidimensional context to the haka and surrounds it with a rich tapestry of action songs, poi, dress, movement and grace.

There are also a number of contemporary spin-offs of the haka, such as mau rākau (weapon drills), which have been used to give confidence to young people and to put them in touch with their ancient traditions. The use of taiaha and short war clubs as part of a physical regime to discipline the minds and bodies of those who take part in mau rākau training sessions is underpinned by haka in its various forms.

In this update I explore the impact of the haka on Māori leaders who have had haka and kapa haka as the continuous backdrop to their lives as they have progressed upwards to the top of their professions or spheres. Some of these like Āpirana Mahuika have had te reo me ōna tikanga (the language and its practice) as an integral part of their lives and come from a long line of gifted whānau. Others like Pita Sharples have fought to overcome early obstacles to become experts in the field of haka and kapa haka. There are many senior Māori leaders who have had as a recurring theme in their lives the focus on, and practice of, haka and kapa haka.

With these objectives in mind it is important for me to acknowledge the role of haka and kapa haka composers. Again I turn to my wife's tribe Ngāti Porou as not only have they produced outstanding composers and compositions, they have also produced leaders like Sir Apirana Ngata who, in his lifetime, was responsible for a renaissance in many aspects of traditional Māori life, not least being in the area of performing arts. Two Ngāti Porou women, Moetū (Tuini) Ngawai and Ngoingoi Pēwhairangi stand out as beacons in the contemporary field of composition.

More recently, others like Archdeacon Kīngi Ihaka, Tīmoti Kāretu, Wiremu Parker, Bub Wehi, Horowaewae (Trevor) Maxwell, Tama Huata, Herewini Parata, Rikirangi Gage, Te Rurehe Rangihau and Te Makarini Te Mara, to name just a few, have all made their mark in the field of kapa haka composition, performance and judging.

In exploring the role of haka and kapa haka in politics I can not think of a more powerful personality than Dr Pita Sharples: an academic, an outstanding exponent of kapa haka, a proponent of Māori representation in Parliament and now the co-leader of the Māori Party in the New Zealand Parliament. It seems astonishing that over the years his is the first comment one reads or hears about when a matter affecting the haka comes up. Throughout this book his name keeps popping up as the 'reasonable' commentator who is bound to give a balanced view on matters relating to haka and kapa haka.

In my earlier book I focused on the role of women in haka and recounted from the historical context observations about women and their roles in haka as seen by early European explorers, visitors and settlers. In this revised version I want to look at the role of Māori women in contemporary haka and kapa haka.

Haka continues to be a vehicle for protest. Perhaps one of the best-known protesters in New Zealand is Tame Iti. His actions in firing a double-barrelled shotgun into the New Zealand flag earned him a court appearance and a guilty verdict for unlawful possession of a firearm in a public place. In April 2007 this decision was overturned by the Court of Appeal. His actions alongside those of members of the Tūhoe tribe, in early 2006, when

Teka Studios, Alexander Turnbull Library, G-16753-1/1-

Children performing haka in the nineteenth century – reminds me of when I was a kid!

they mounted a vigorous and colourful protest against the Crown, capture the full intensity of haka being used as an expression of anger and a weapon of political theatre.

Like many Māori, I have grown up watching or performing haka. As a young person, I belonged to a group that performed haka for tourists. Ever since then I have been a part of — sometimes directly and sometimes as an observer — the growing phenomenon of the haka. During my lifetime, the growth in interest in haka reflects the parallel renaissance of Māori in reclaiming their heritage from the brink of cultural extinction. It also reflects the substantial efforts made to bridge the gulf that lies between Māori and Pākehā Aotearoa New Zealanders. It seems ironic that Aotearoa New Zealanders have become increasingly attached to this dramatic form of a previous time as a means of expressing our pride as Aotearoa New Zealanders in the new century.

These days, I am a keen social observer of the haka. Nevertheless I can still call to mind the range of experiences and responses from my youth when I was a semi-active participant in various haka parties. While the sight and sound of a well-executed haka raises the hackles on my neck and the temptation to leap up briefly crosses my mind, the reality is that the body stays firmly fixed in the chair.

Tīmoti Kāretu, the Chairman of the Aotearoa Traditional Māori Performing Arts Society during the 1990s, and I share one experience in common: we have both seen the performance of unconventional or bastardised forms of traditional haka in our younger days. Tīmoti's experience of this was as a student at Wellington College, while mine was as an army cadet at the Royal Military College, Duntroon, Australia. Our reactions differed. He rebelled against any form of participation in what he saw as shallow debasement of the traditional haka style and philosophy, which must have been difficult given the very strong peer pressure from other students. On the other hand, I not only took part in leading the college haka but I rejoiced in doing so.

My own experiences of the haka came in five distinct phases of my life. When I was a youngster, growing up at Hinehopu, on the eastern shores of Lake Rotoiti, I belonged to

a local concert party that entertained tourists. The tourists crossed the lake by launch from the Rotorua side, stayed for lunch and were entertained by our concert party. I can't say that my recollections of this time include distinct memories of actually performing the haka. If the truth be known, I and my young relatives around five to ten years of age filled in the gaps and gave the party a family look about it — an important aspect of entertainment with overseas tourists clicking their cameras!

My next involvement with haka came in my late teens and early twenties when I attended the four-year officer training course at the Royal Military College, Duntroon. Aotearoa New Zealand had a long, almost unbroken association with the college since its inception in 1911 and many of the senior officers of the New Zealand Army had been trained there.

Between 1963 and 1966 when I was a cadet there we more often than not reached the grand finals of the Canberra rugby union competition. These were years when rugby was truly an amateur game and the Australian sides had yet to reach the level of the South Africans or All Blacks and indeed had some way to go before achieving the levels of supremacy they have today.

Grand final day was a fantastic affair and before our college First XV ran onto the field a couple of hundred cadets lined up to perform the college haka. I don't know who introduced the haka to Duntroon but it was an emasculated version of the haka 'Ka Mate!'. Notwithstanding its lack of authenticity, it certainly sent shivers down our spines and gave our team the psychological advantage — at least that's what we thought! I can't remember us winning too many grand finals, however. On reflection I don't know what stopped me from simply replacing the college version of the haka with the real thing. Maybe it was just a case of tradition overriding accuracy.

My next encounter with haka came as a young officer serving in Malaysia in 1968. Aotearoa New Zealanders had been serving in Malaysia since 1957 (when it was known as Malaya) and had deployed from there to fight in Borneo against the Indonesians and subsequently from 1967 on to South Vietnam. The Aotearoa New Zealand Battalion serving in Malaysia had always had a concert party, and the head of the party at the time was a Major Alan Armstrong, who had co-authored with Reupena Ngata the comprehensive book *Māori Action Songs*.[1]

Alan had gained a lot of his knowledge of haka dances and songs from the Ngāti Porou tribe on the East Coast. He had married Wai Te Ua, a granddaughter of Sir Apirana Ngata, the Ngāti Porou leader and long-serving politician who was responsible for leading the revitalisation of Māori society during the 1920s and 1930s. Ngāti Porou people were then, and still are, famous for their capacity to launch immediately into haka and song at a moment's notice. Not surprisingly, the haka and songs we sang and danced came largely from Ngāti Porou and in particular the haka 'Rūaumoko'. Some members of the concert party became adept at presenting other tribes' items without a full understanding of their words or significance.

What we did know and feel was the power of doing a haka in a disciplined and highly coordinated manner. The projection of controlled aggression during the haka accompanied by the pūkana (enlarging the whites of the eyes and distorting one's features to appear fierce) had a great impact on the crowds that came to watch us perform.

In 1989 I was appointed to head the Iwi Transition Agency (the remains of the old Department of Māori Affairs minus the Māori Land Court, which had been transferred to the Justice Department). I invited a number of elders from the tribes I am descended from

to form a support group for me and to advise me on a wide range of cultural issues.

The group, known as Ngā Tuarā (the backbone), included Professor Hirini Mead of Victoria University, a key leader of our tribe Ngāti Awa; Te Makarini Temara, a senior tribal leader from Tūhoe; Bishop Manu Bennett and Kāwana Nēpia, both elders and leaders of the Te Arawa tribe from which I am descended, and Keita Walker from Ngāti Porou, who is related to me on my mother's side from Te Whānau-a-Apanui (she is the younger sister of Second-Lieutenant Moananui-a-kiwa Ngarimu who was posthumously awarded the Victoria Cross for bravery at Tebaga Gap, Tunisia, in 1943). The role of this group was to shepherd me through some of the complex shoals of Māori society.

One of our first official visits in 1999 was to Ngāti Awa, in Whakatāne, the tribe to whom I owe my primary affiliation. We were welcomed onto Taiwhakaea marae and, as we moved on to the marae (gathering place), one of Ngāti Awa's leading elders and tohunga (spiritual advisors), Te Hau Tutua, leapt out and commenced a short haka:

Hōri Pawa tōia te ure	Hōri Pawa pulls his penis
Hōri Pawa tōia te ure	Hōri Pawa pulls his penis
Kei te Māpou rā te ure toa	The brave warrior's penis is at Māpou
Ka pau tō ringa te tītoi	Your hand will tire from the pulling
Kirikiri korehe i aha hā!	The skin will shrivel [shrink] alas!

I was taken by surprise when I heard my great-grandfather's name being used in the haka. The haka is an uncomplimentary description of the philandering escapades of my great-grandfather around 1900.

Subsequently, I asked Hirini Mead (an expert in Māori culture and society) what had given rise to the haka. He explained that the haka composed about my great-grandfather Hōri Pawa (George Powell) had probably been written at the time when he left his first wife and married another woman. In the late nineteenth and early twentieth centuries Hōri Pawa had worked with the Native Land Court. It was suggested that he had somehow used his position to obtain land that did not belong to him.

There are always stories of this kind in any family. It struck me as remarkable that a short haka lasting no more than half a minute could be retained as part of tribal heritage and kept for use on the appropriate occasion, which might not be for many, many years. It shows the great qualities of tribal tohunga that they can store this kind of information and perform it to mark a particular occasion.

Notwithstanding its less than complimentary content, the haka was an acknowledgement that Hōri Pawa was a significant character from our tribal past and, because I was his direct descendant, it was deemed a suitable occasion to perform this mark of recognition. Far from being embarrassed by this somewhat arcane ditty from our tribal history, I was very pleased that my great-grandfather's name was still alive in the tribal memory. The incident further reinforced for me that a disaster in one context can later be seen in a very different light by observers of another time and place.

In the same year I was privileged to visit Ruatāhuna, the isolated and majestically beautiful valley settlement of the Tūhoe people. When I arrived there my entourage was met with rows of men and women of all ages and sizes and as we moved onto the marae we were thrilled with one of Tūhoe's traditional haka, 'Ko te Pūru'. It was a deeply moving and challenging haka that generations of Tūhoe have learned and performed. In this small

community hidden from most Aotearoa New Zealanders' gaze and access, I discovered the deeply primal sense that comes from witnessing an ancestral treasure that has been passed down through time.

Over the last 15 years my involvement with haka has been mostly through observing my wife's tribe, Ngāti Porou. At a number of functions we have attended, and following key speeches, I have been struck by the way in which nearly all members of this tribe readily identify with and can take part in the many waiata and haka that follow speeches. I have seen this happen on numerous occasions. In Wainuiomata in 2002 we attended a social function at which there were about 200 people. I must have been one of the few non-Ngāti Porou people in the crowd. After one particular speech by Dr Tamati Reedy (recently retired as Vice-Chancellor (Māori) at Waikato University) I observed the remarkable spectacle of all able-bodied men in a room immediately surging forward to the call to perform the haka 'Rūaumoko'. The spontaneity, the unanimity of purpose and the ability to immediately join the cadence of the haka was a joy to behold, although it might have been quite intimidating to the uninitiated. It showed me the powerful tribal bonding that can be achieved through the constant practice and performance of tribal haka.

In my own tribe, Ngāti Awa, I have not observed to the same extent the spontaneity of haka that I have seen in other tribes. That is not to say that we do not have haka experts; indeed, we have highly acclaimed individuals. Te Hau Tutua, for example, is widely acknowledged throughout Māoridom for his expertise as a tohunga and as an exponent of the haka. Also, my nephew Pouroto Ngāropo, a young man of extraordinary talents, has recently emerged as a tohunga.

In recent years the building and maintenance of waka (canoes) has seen a number of tribes like mine foster a spirit of camaraderie and teamwork. This has as its focus the chants and haka necessary to prepare the warriors for carrying and removing the waka from the water and for ensuring teamwork and coordination on the water. The resurgence of haka in our tribe seems to stem from the efforts of the kaihoe (rowers) and their leaders to reach the highest pinnacle of excellence in their readiness for the duties associated with crewing and caring for our waka.

Who can forget the 1990 celebrations at Waitangi? The tribes assembled and a number brought with them their waka. It was an awe-inspiring sight to watch hundreds of young warriors assembling on the beach at Waitangi to board their waka for the day's activities. Before they boarded and when they disembarked

Te Whānau-a-Apanui, winners of Te Matatini 2005 performing 'The dance of the Moki fish' (prized fish of the tribe).

Courtesy of Te Whānau-a-Apanui Kapa Haka and Te Matatini. Photographer Aaron Smale

Te Whānau-a-Apanui: Placed fifth in 2007.

each group performed a haka. The trampling of feet on the sand and the use of the oar blades as 'weapons' in their respective haka reminded observers of another age.

Ngāti Awa had carved a waka for the occasion. The enterprise was led by Pene Mamaku, who trained the crews and over the years has maintained within our tribe the waka traditions of our ancestors, which for many of us have become a blurred, distant memory. In 1993, when Hekia Parata and I were married at Waiomatatini on the East Coast, Pene and his waka crew were travelling to take part in a waka festival. They detoured to my wedding and put on a truly spectacular performance of haka and waiata that made me proud of my Ngāti Awa heritage.

Since my retirement from the Public Service in 1995, I have attended the Aotearoa Traditional Māori Performing Arts Festival (now Te Matatini Festival) a couple of times through the kind invitation of the Chief Executive, Doug Hauraki, and have been amazed at the huge numbers of Māori that turn out for these biennial events. It is on these occasions, and at the preliminary regional competitions, that one can plumb the depths of interest in kapa haka (haka groups).

In the past I have observed that there appeared to be little difference between the top performing groups. While the levels of competence were consistently high, the performances, because of their similarity, did not stretch or excite the imagination as much. However, over the past few years I have noticed a movement of groups towards a recapturing of traditional styles and dress.

I was in Tauranga in 1998 with some relatives watching the televised finals of the Aotearoa Traditional Māori Performing Arts Festival. We watched the finalist groups parade on stage and go through their items while we continued chatting, and it was as if the performers formed a surreal backdrop to our conversation. Suddenly we all stopped talking and turned to the television when a group called Te Mātārae-i-o-Rehu, of Ngāti Pikiao, came on the stage. They were a striking group, and in their dress and movements they evoked memories of a long-distant past. Their performance was stunning and we all agreed we had seen a watershed event, and that the festival would not be the same again.

The group did not win but came a creditable third place and, in doing so, broke into the top ranks of the best performers. It was thus no surprise to us all when they won in 2000, beating the fancied contenders who had dominated the festival for a number of years. Seeing them perform is like watching and listening to our ancestors.

In 2001 I saw an example of the awesome power of combining the traditional haka and dance of Te Mātārae-i-o-Rehu with modern, choreographed sequences by dancers of the Aotearoa New Zealand Ballet Company set to the music of Neil Finn. The Māori group, in its urgency, projection of power and energy, was fantastic. I could see in my mind's eye my Ngāti Pikiao relation Irirangi Tiakiwā, the group's founder who died some years ago, in the way in which they presented themselves and their items. I could see our ancestors coming alive with their routines. The sheer physicality of their leaders Wētini-Mītai Ngātai and Taini Morrison drove the group in its efforts to reach greater heights of excellence.

Regrettably in recent years the group has become a victim of the internecine politics that can happen in any organisation. For the last two Te Matatini festivals the major Te Arawa groups have declined to attend the kapa haka festival on the grounds that they objected to the way in which the festival was proceeding.

In 2005 another group emerged to win the hearts and minds of Māori audiences. The Te Whānau-a-Apanui group from my mother's tribal area, the narrow strip of land between the sea and the mountain ranges in the Eastern Bay of Plenty, demonstrated that kapa haka need not be about shouting and yelling, and trying to scream your way into first place. Their relatively relaxed style, their reliance on their own deep traditions and their innovative but highly appealing item around the catching of their favourite sea fish, the Moki, captured the imaginations of the judges and the audience.

My own experiences are probably similar to many Māori, who have been at the edge of, and sometimes in the thick of, haka action. Most would share my feelings, though, that haka is an inescapable and vital part of our culture, one that reminds us who we are and of those who have come before.

'Haka Boogie' — the battalion concert party

The Aotearoa New Zealand Army served in Malaya (now Malaysia) to combat a Communist insurgency from 1957 to 1961. The Aotearoa New Zealand Battalion formed a concert party, which was used as part of the British and Aotearoa New Zealand strategy of communicating with Malayans, especially in isolated rural communities. As a soldier, the only way one could be excused duties from jungle training was to be a member of the battalion rugby team or a member of the concert party — known affectionately and not without a little bit of jealousy by the soldiers of the battalion as 'Haka Boogie'.

The battalion concert party went on frequent tours around Malaya, and the haka was a central item of the programme. Chinese Malayans especially used to revel in the spectacle. When we stamped and rocked the temporary stages on which we performed, they responded with eyes opened wide with excitement and not a little fear at the contorted faces, protruding tongues, and the slapping of thighs and chests. It was quite an eerie feeling to keep the cadence while performing some feet above the ground on a flimsy stage which seemed to sway as we performed!

Haka in legend

Ra and Hine-raumati lay together and gave birth to a son called Tanerore. On hot summer days it is possible to see the light dancing. Legend has it that this is Hine-raumati's son, Tanerore, performing for his mother, and the wiriwiri or trembling shimmer is today reflected in the trembling of the haka performer's hands. The haka is often referred to as 'the dance of Tanerore: the quivering of the air on a hot day'.

Māori myths and legends have numerous references to haka, and the legends related here are just a few of the better known in relation to haka.

The first application of the haka in the mortal world was attributed to the chief Tinirau and some of his womenfolk.[1]

Tradition from Polynesia

Tinirau and Kae

The chief Tinirau wanted to bless the child Tūhuruhuru so that he would be a successful warrior and so Tinirau sought out the best tohunga in the area to carry out the deed. The old tohunga Kae came to Tinirau's village and blessed the child. Tinirau wanted to reward Kae with something special and called his pet whale Tutunui to shore. The whale arrived and Tinirau cut off a piece of it, cooked it and then gave it to Kae. Kae found it delicious and wanted more.

When it came time for Kae to return to his village he tarried and declined the offer of a waka to take him home. Eventually Tinirau said to Kae that he could ride home on his pet whale. Kae quickly agreed to this and, after receiving instructions on how to mount and dismount the whale, set off home. However, when he reached his home village he did not dismount but instead remained on the whale's back. Tutunui fought and bucked but to no avail. Eventually his blowhole was blocked up with sand and he died.

Kae's people beached the whale and cut him up into pieces, which they put into hāngī (oven) pits to cook. They laid the branches of the koromiko tree on top of the meat to give it fragrance and then piled sand on top of the branches to allow the meat to cook. The fat of the whale stuck to the leaves and branches and hence today when one uses branches of the koromiko as part of a hāngī and they become greasy, it is said that some of the taste of Tutunui the pet whale has rubbed off.

Tinirau very soon missed his pet whale and mounted a search for it. However, he and his wife smelled the scent of whale meat wafting across the seas and they realised what had happened. Tinirau sent a party of 40 women to hunt for Kae as they would be least likely to raise his

Manu Smith in Bacon, Ron, *Tinirau and His Whale*, (pp. 2–3), Waiatarua Publishing, Auckland, 1995

Chief Tinirau riding his pet whale Tutunui.

suspicion. Although the women did not know what he looked like, they knew that his teeth were uneven and they overlapped one another. The agreed strategy was that they should make him laugh in order to recognise him by his crooked teeth.

When the hunting party arrived at Kae's village the women tried to humour the crowd by playing games and music, but they failed to get the onlookers to laugh. One woman then got up and danced with exaggerated movements. The audience laughed at these antics and Kae's smile gave him away. He was thus identified, overcome with karakia or incantations and captured. He was taken back to Tinirau's village and later killed.

So it was that the haka taparahi (haka performed without weapons) was used for the first time. However, even in death the old tohunga had the last laugh. His tribe rose up, attacked Tinirau's village and killed Tinirau's son. There are numerous other examples in Māori traditional history where the haka was used as a means to distract watchers, in some cases facilitating an escape. One of the tribes I belong to is Ngāti Pikiao. The tribe is centred on Lake Rotoiti. We belong to the Te Arawa confederation of tribes, which derives its name from the ancestral waka *Te Arawa*, which sailed to Aotearoa out of Polynesia as part of the early settlement of this country. The captain of the *Te Arawa* waka was Tamatekapua and this next legend concerns him and his younger brother, Whakatūria.[2]

Te Arawa tradition

Tamatekapua and Whakatūria

In their ancestral homelands before coming to Aotearoa New Zealand, Tamatekapua and his younger brother Whakatūria set out to steal breadfruit from the tree of the village owned by a powerful chief called Uenuku. They used stilts to get to the fruit but they were caught in the act of stealing it. They attempted to escape and while Tamatekapua was successful in getting away, Whakatūria was captured.

Whakatūria was taken to the main meeting house and was strung up in the rafters, where he was taunted by the villagers as he suffered from the smoke rising from the fire below him. Tamatekapua waited until dark and then climbed up onto the roof. He punched a hole through the thatching and whispered to his brother. Together they planned a way to get Whakatūria out of his predicament.

As the people gathered for the night and dances were performed, Whakatūria called out from above that their performances were substandard and that he could do much better than they could at haka. The people below were incensed, but at

Kumete-carved wooden bowl depicts Tamatekapua and Whakatūria stealing from Uenuku with the help of their dog.

the same time intrigued by this challenge so they brought Whakatūria down. He persuaded them to clean him up and to give him a weapon so that he could dance properly.

As he began it quickly became clear that he was surely an exponent of the haka. As he danced they became mesmerised by his performance. He asked them to open the door to let in fresh air and they did. As he did his haka he moved imperceptibly towards the door, and when he got close to the door he darted out. Together with his brother Tamatekapua, he made a safe getaway.

Uenuku, enraged by the escape, attacked Tamatekapua's village and threatened to overrun it. However, with the help of his father, Houmaitawhiti, Tamatekapua was able to destroy Uenuku's army.

Shortly after this incident Tamatekapua decided to leave the island and seek out other lands. Subsequently, Tamatekapua led a group of his people on the voyage to Aotearoa New Zealand. He and his brother are remembered through the names given to the elaborate meeting house, Tamatekapua, and the dining hall, Whakatūria, at Ōhinemutu in Rotorua.

Ngati Raukawa tradition

The Wairangi haka

Some centuries later, from Ngāti Raukawa, a tribal group belonging to the Tainui confederation of tribes,[4] comes another example of the use of the haka to beguile the audience and so mask the real intent of the haka party. The haka was composed by one of the grandsons of Raukawa, a chief called Wairangi. At the heart of the composition of this haka lay a wife's infidelity.

Tūpeteka, a chief of the Ngāti Maru tribe in the Waikato, called to visit his relative Parawhete, who was one of the wives of Wairangi, a Ngāti Raukawa chief. While Wairangi was absent, Tūpeteka had an affair with Parawhete. On his return Wairangi was angered to be told that one of his wives had been unfaithful. He beat her and she ran away to her lover's village at Te Aea, near present-day Te Aroha, where she married him.

Ngāti Raukawa organised themselves to exact revenge and sent a war party to Tūpeteka's village. In the war party were Wairangi and his three brothers: Tamatehura, Upokoiti and Pipito. The Ngāti Maru people welcomed them, but the visitors were warned, ironically by Wairangi's wife, Parawhete, that Tūpeteka's people actually intended to kill them. So, the Ngāti Raukawa warriors decided to do a haka, at the end of which they would launch a surprise attack on Tūpeteka's people.

The four brothers each agreed to compose a short haka and then perform it. Wairangi's three brothers preceded him and the local Ngāti Maru people watched admiringly, entranced by the performance and lulled into relaxing their vigilance.

As the haka of the last brother, Wairangi, drew to a close Wairangi's warriors pulled out their weapons and attacked Ngāti Maru. They showed no mercy and killed Tūpeteka and all his people. The sole survivor of the carnage was Parawhete, who was forgiven by her husband and taken back to Wairangi's pā.

Wairangi haka

The noted Māori historian Pei Te Hurinui Jones describes below the performance of the Wairangi haka.[3]

The haka begins with the warriors kneeling on their left knee.

The first warrior leader rises, holding a toki (adze); he calls out his words and then sinks to the ground, and buries the toki.

The next warrior leader rises. He is armed with a double-pointed spear, some three metres or more long. After completing his words, which are supported by the kneeling warriors, he too subsides.

The third warrior leader rises, armed with a mere or short jabbing club.

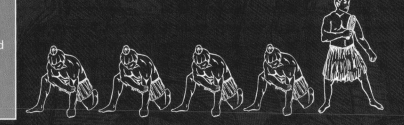

When he reaches the word huakina ('charge') the rest of the warriors rise to their feet. Wairangi now takes command and completes the haka, after which they fall upon the hapless Ngāti Maru.

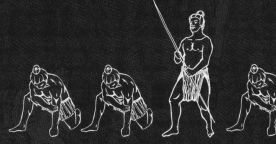

21

Elsdon Best once observed that it was very difficult to translate traditional haka into English as many of the words used had particular meanings according to their context and depending also on which tribe used it. Nevertheless, when reading the translations of some of the traditional and ancient haka it is best to try to visualise the event and then read the translation generally, rather than trying to mine for specific meaning. Therefore, when reading the translation below of the Ngāti Raukawa haka it is easy to imagine the build-up of preparedness of Wairangi's group and the growing relaxation of Tūpeteka's people.

Tamatehura:	Ko Te Aea o ia rangi, ko Te Aea o ia rangi, hui ake!	Tamatehura:	Te Aea of everyday fame, of everyday fame, gather here!
Te Nuinga:	Ko Te Aea o ia rangi, o ia rangi, o ia rangi!	Chorus:	Te Aea of everyday fame, of everyday fame, of everyday fame!
Upokoiti:	Ka whakakōpura Ruarangi-hape, teina o Tūpeteka e-e!	Upokoiti:	Ruarangi-hape, younger brother of Tūpeteka, dazzles like the Morning Star!
Te Nuinga:	O Tūpeteka e! O Tūpeteka e!	Chorus:	Tūpeteka! Tūpeteka!
Upokoiti:	Huakina!	Upokoiti:	Charge!
Te Nuinga:	Huakina! huakina!	Chorus:	Charge! Charge!
Pipito:	Puhi kura, puhi kura, puhi kākā! Ka whakatautapa ki Kāwhia. Huakina!	Pipito:	Red plumes! Red plumes! Parrot plumes challenging Kāwhia! Charge!
Te Nuinga:	Huakina! Huakina!	Chorus:	Charge! Charge!
Wairangi:	Kātahi ka riri, i toru ka whā. Matamata, hopukia!	Wairangi:	Now fight. Three, four Matamata, seize him!
Te Nuinga:	Hōmai rā tō whiri kaha, toro kaha, ka wetewetea, ka wetewetea. Ā-tē! Ā-tā! Ā-tau.	Chorus:	Give here your strong ropes, your vines to be unravelled, unravelled. They are unfastened, unfastened, unfastened!

And so the memory of the manner in which Ngāti Raukawa exacted their revenge is preserved in this haka, one that is still performed today on suitable occasions.

Haka variations

The nature of haka

The word haka is defined in H W Williams' *A Dictionary of the Māori Language* as 'a dance'.[1] Another meaning given is: 'song, accompanying a dance'. Both these definitions are technically correct, although they seem to squeeze the mauri (or life force) from what is such a vigorous artform.

When asked to define the haka, most people will identify it as a war dance. This is an erroneous description, but it is an understandable one given that most contemporary non-Māori have in minds a picture of the haka 'Ka Mate!' performed by the All Blacks and other sports teams, with its accompanying air of aggression.

Alan Armstrong, a Pākehā who mastered the Māori language and then went on to write about Māori and their songs and haka, described the essence of haka as:

> . . . *[a] composition played by many instruments. Hands, feet, legs, body, voice, tongue, and eyes all play their part in blending together to convey in their fullness the challenge, welcome, exultation, defiance or contempt of the words.*[2]

In his writings on Māori music, Johannes C Andersen noted that:

> . . . *the haka . . . was intended not only to intimidate the enemy, but also to work up the performer to the pitch of excitement necessary to enable him to 'go over the top'. When worked up to the proper pitch he was insensible to the 'odd hits' . . . and if his opponent, his 'angry friend' [hoariri], felt them, well, the entrance to Te Reinga was wide, and was never closed.*[3]

Te Rēinga, at the northernmost tip of the North Island, is the departure point to the underworld for the spirits of those who have died.

In his book *The Coming of the Māori*, Sir Peter Buck described haka as 'posture dancing', which was exemplified by the:

> . . . *energetic movements of hands and feet with the accompanying ferocity of facial expressions heightened by glaring eyes and protruding tongue.*[4]

The haka peruperu — Ngāti Tūwharetoa in full flight at Waitangi, 1934.

Buck said that the words used by the performers

> *. . . were composed to meet various social events but, though the performances were peaceful in intent, they had to be demonstrated with energy and sound to make the welcome truly hearty.*

Te Hāmana Mahuika, a Ngāti Porou expert on the haka, also commented on its social role:

> *The haka, however, was not merely a pastime, but it was also a custom of high social importance in the welcoming and entertainment of visitors. Tribal reputation often rose or fell on their ability to perform the haka. The leader had to be an expert, who, by the timing of voice and movement, influenced the performance of his team.*[5]

Haka types

When consulting experts on the haka and reviewing recent and historical literature, a common theme is that there are many variations of haka and the distinctions between them are easily blurred. The nature of the haka has altered over time to reflect the changing nature of Māori society and its interactions with European society over more than 366 years. The impact of these changes has seen a fall-off in the numbers and types of haka being performed, as well as the loss of expertise for many of the variations described in this chapter when they ceased to have utility or purpose.

Mervyn McLean and Margaret Orbell in *Traditional Songs of the Māori* noted that, in pre-European times, there were many kinds of haka, including those performed for amusement, those for welcoming visitors, and some used as war dances.[6]

Armstrong describes two general types of haka: *haka taparahi*, which is performed 'without weapons and may express any public or private sentiment', and *haka peruperu*, in which the performers carry weapons.[7] He further defines all haka as subsets of these two main groups depending on their purpose.

According to Armstrong, in the peruperu group are dances and songs that should most properly be called war dances, as they were performed by warriors as part of the process of preparing for battle. They were also used as a way to celebrate victories. Haka taparahi, on the other hand, are 'shouted posture dances . . . generally performed today'. They include the haka 'Ka Mate!'.

As well as being distinguished by whether weapons are carried or not, haka can also be differentiated by whether or not they are performed with uniform movements. Most haka fall into the category of being performed in a uniform manner. However, there are some haka where performers have licence to improvise their actions. In his book *Māori Music* Mervyn McLean observes that the distinction which Armstrong suggests

> . . . is tidy but is certainly wrong for peruperu and is true of haka taparahi only in so far as Armstrong's judgement has been adopted by others . . . It appears to have resulted from misunderstanding. The haka taparahi is indeed performed without weapons, but so are numerous other forms of haka that are not taparahi.[8]

McLean's preference is to describe types of haka by their function, by their manner of performance, by grouping of performers and by a group which he describes as funeral compositions in haka style.[9] These are described further on pages 30–31.

Haka peruperu and the 'true' war dances

Lieutenant-Colonel Arapeta Awatere, the eccentrically brilliant fighting chief of Ngāti Porou who led the 28th (Māori) Battalion towards the end of the Second World War, was a renowned expert on the haka. He said that the peruperu was the true war dance, and noted that:

> Peruperu is the intensive form of peru 'anger' and this is how the war-dance got its name, and that is its psychological purpose which no other form of haka could match in the past, can match now, nor ever will.[10]

McLean describes three types of war dances:[11]
- **Haka peruperu**, in which the warriors jump up with legs tucked under them
- **Haka puha**, a Te Arawa haka which was used to prepare warriors for battle
- **Tūtūngārahu**, a Waikato war dance which was used to prepare warriors for battle. Variations of this type of war dance include the following:
  - *Whakatūwaewae*, a Ngāti Porou war dance similar to tūtūngārahu
  - *Tūngārahu*, a Ngāpuhi and Ngāti Porou war dance
  - *Ngārahu*, a Te Arawa and Ngāpuhi war dance
  - *Whakarewarewa*, a Te Arawa war dance before battle.

Alexander Turnbull Library, PUBL–0033-1866-417

The massed ranks of Ngāi Te Rangi performing a haka peruperu at Tauranga in 1865.

While there are variations between the types of war dance the common feature is that they are all performed with weapons. Today these weapons are generally replicas of those used for war in pre-European times and during the nineteenth century. In recent cultural competitions some teams have performed haka peruperu with replicas of muskets. As described later, members of the Tūhoe tribe at times carry and discharge double-barrelled shotguns on important occasions.

Armstrong describes the importance of the haka peruperu in battle preparations. Prior to leaving for battle, a war party would assemble on the marae. Here they would perform the tūtūngārahu, one of the variations of the haka peruperu, designed as an inspection of the troops before battle. During the performance of the haka

> . . . *elders would bend low and watch the feet. All performers had to be in the air together in the tremendous leaps of the haka, for disunity in the dance was an omen of disaster to follow.*[12]

This theme was reinforced by Tuta Nihoniho. Nihoniho was an officer in the Ngāti Porou native contingent that fought alongside the British and colonial troops during the land wars of the 1860s and 1870s. He was the author of a remarkable essay written to describe the preparation of warriors for war. The essay was translated into English by Augustus Hamilton[13] who called Nihoniho's essay 'a mixture of exceedingly good advice to young soldiers and explanations of curious Native beliefs in divers omens'.

In his essay Nihoniho exhorted young men readying for war to not forget their ancestor Uenuku:

. . . the god of your forefathers, by whose help they crossed the Great Ocean of Kiwa that lies before us. The first item for consideration as an omen is in regard to the direction of affairs.

Nihoniho then enumerates a number of important steps that warriors must go through in preparation for war. The first of these steps related to the manner in which they prepared themselves through haka:

Ere you go forth to fight display your legs to your women [according to Hamilton this means strip and perform the war dance], young folk, and old men in what is termed a war-dance. Your women will never fail to observe the omens of the dance — the correctness of attitudes or mistakes committed. When your women are seen by you advancing with distorted faces by the side of your column, or columns, the rising of Tu-te-ihiihi, of Tu-te-wanawana (the war god), you then know that your legs will assail the stars in the heavens and the earth mother below.

In his notes to the essay Hamilton observes that the expression 'your legs will assail the stars' means that if there is an absence of any omens during the haka preparation then victory can be assured. Thus it was important for the warriors to be highly disciplined in their actions and it was especially important, as observed earlier, that when their legs left the ground in any leaps they must be of uniform height and there must not be any lazy or uncoordinated movements.

The price for any errors was dire according to Nihoniho:

But should you commit errors and not deport yourself correctly, then assuredly you will not see your women dancing and grimacing, because apprehension has seized them, for from them comes the blood of the performing men that is to be borne into the fray and poured forth upon the land. So then you are aware that an error has been made in your dancing, therefore be cautious — it is a malignant demon (the devil to pay) — wait and see if the evil omen does not pass by; or look carefully at your ancestor Uenuku [a war god symbolised by a rainbow], who will urge you on or restrain you. Should he be seen by you standing in the form of a bow over the track behind you as you face your enemy, go on, for that is the time when your enemy will be delivered into your hand by the god.

According to Best, during the haka peruperu,

. . . should any man not keep time with the others, or not leap so high, these also were korapa and evil omens. When called on to arise by the leader, should the warriors rise in perfect time — all together — that is a kura takahi puni and a good omen. But if some are slow to rise, and lag behind, this is a hawaiki pepeke, and an evil omen for the expedition.[14]

Elsdon Best noted that the haka peruperu was performed in three situations.[15] The first was on the arrival of a company of visitors. Part of the ritual of encounter (which will be described in the next chapter) was based on the assumption that the intentions of the

visiting party were unknown. Therefore, the war party's preparedness and the war dance accompanying the ritual helped determine the status of the visitors — whether they came in peace or whether they came to wage battle.

The second situation was when the war party was preparing to go to war or immediately before a battle. In this case the peruperu or war dance was performed to determine whether the gods of war were sympathetic to the kaupapa (or purpose) of the expedition. The performance by the warriors of the peruperu helped the tribal tohunga to determine the omens and try to divine whether success or defeat lay ahead of them.

The third situation when the haka peruperu was performed was on the battlefield at the successful conclusion of a battle, after the enemy had fled the field. The war dance allowed the victors to trumpet their success, thus demonstrating their superiority and the joy of victory.

Like all sensible religious practices, if the omens were not propitious then the chiefs and spiritual leaders whose task it was to read the signs would demand a repeat performance; this process was called the tuora, the practice to gain better omens. If the repeat performance had no errors this was called waiora, and the war party could proceed to war or engage in battle.

Age shall not weary . . . Ngāti Tūwharetoa perform a peruperu at Tūrangi in the nineteenth century.

Despite the cessation of wars between Māori and Māori, and between Māori and the British imperial regiments and colonial troops, the practice of the haka peruperu has not diminished. While the penalties are no longer as severe as in pre-European times and the nineteenth century for the failure to faultlessly perform a haka peruperu, the desire of contemporary kapa haka parties to attain perfection remains.

The prize nowadays is not the security of going to war or entering into battle with the appropriate spiritual omens on the side of the war party, rather the satisfaction now lies with impressing judges on the flawlessness of the performance to ensure the victor captures the prize of first place in a cultural competition.

Other haka

As mentioned, McLean questions Armstrong's grouping together as haka taparahi those haka that are not clearly haka peruperu. The other types of haka described by McLean include the following:

Haka described by function

- **Ngeri**, any short informal composition in haka form performed with or without dance that can be regarded as a short, sharp, wake-up action
- **Tūtara or kōtaratara**, a type of ngeri in which words use sexual connotations and imagery to express derision
- **Tumoto**, another type of ngeri which is a virulent chant to indicate revenge for some injury or defeat in battle
- **Pīrori**, a haka performed naked which indicats contempt and revulsion
- **Kaioraora**, a haka composed by women to vent their anger at an event which has occurred

Haka described by manner of performance

- **Haka horuhoru**, performed in a kneeling position by both sexes
- **Haka horiri**, performed with swaying movements
- **Haka matohi**, performed by men only in which they exaggeratedly expose their posterior
- **Haka pikari**, in which feet are shuffled

Haka described by grouping of performers

- **Haka aroākapa**, a haka performed in two ranks
- **Haka porowhā**, a haka in which performers are arranged in a square

Tūhoe delegation perform for Premier Richard Seddon, Wellington, 1890s.

Funeral compositions
- **Haka maemae or maimai**, a haka performed to welcome guests to a tangi
- **Haka manawawera**, a haka traditionally performed by the Tūhoe tribe in which relatives of those slain in battle vilify the returning war party
- **Haka pihe,** a haka performed by the northern tribes and similar to maemae and manawawera
- **Haka pōkeka**, a haka performed by Te Arawa, again similar to maemae and manawawera

Other types
- **Haka poi,** in which the poi ball is used
- **Haka pōwhiri,** a haka of welcome performed by women before the men move forward to do a haka taparahi
- **Haka tūtohu**, performed as a divinatory exercise by persons grouped in a wedge formation
- **Haka waiata**, the forerunner of the modern action song

Making sense of it all!

The many and subtle variations tend to confuse all but the expert and today fewer types of haka are performed. The haka that are performed fall into categories that are clearly recognisable and that have particular relevance for modern kapa haka performances. Now it is only a small number of experts who keep the knowledge and traditions alive.

William Andrews Collis, Alexander Turnbull Library, G-31309½-1/1

Tāre Waitara and party performing a haka horuhoru (kneeling haka) at Parihaka in the 1890s.

A caution against trying to typecast one form of performance into one of the categories described in this chapter is provided by the example of a *pātere* (an action song) from Te Whakatōhea of the Eastern Bay of Plenty that describes a series of battles between them and the neighbouring tribe, Ngāi Tai, residing at Tōrere. After facing two defeats Te Whakatōhea went to see a seer and asked him to divine their chances for the future. The seer told Te Whakatōhea that they would be eventually victorious if they killed all the descendants of Te Whakatōhea who had married into Ngāi Tai, as this would appease the god Tama-i-waho. Te Whakatōhea carried out the seer's instructions and when they next met Ngāi Tai they were victorious.

In 1924 Koopu Eruiti, an elder and chief of Te Whānau-a-Apanui, described the pātere and explained its meaning to Sir Āpirana Ngata. It is quite a lengthy pātere of 76 lines. Ngata describes its performance:

> *This (the Pātere) was accompanied with appropriate hand movements, moving hips and turning heads; and at certain parts the eyes give the defiant or haughty stare, the chorus joins in and the singers seek to excel one another in singing and generally to impart an air of exultation and elation to their performance. Almost, but not quite, the performance becomes a haka (chanted posture dance), but a certain subtle restraint is necessary so as to permit clear enunciation of the words of a kaioraora (threatening, cursing or taunting song).*[16]

In this one composition we have elements of action song, haka and kaioraora (or cursing song).

Kennedy Warne

Modern warriors performing haka with tongues protruding and fierce eye movements (pūkana).

Facial expressions

An integral part of the haka is the range of expressions used by performers. The eyes and the tongue are key components of the haka and their appropriate use by experts can mean the difference between a good haka and one of extraordinary excellence.

The pūkana or dilation of the eyes, the practice of rolling back the eyes so that only the whites are shown, and the whētero, the protruding of the tongue and its movement into and out of the mouth, give a fearsome image to the haka.

Other traditional terms used to describe the range of expressions include:

- **whakatea**, showing the whites of the eyes
- **whakapī**, contorting the body and features
- **weru**, pouting or projecting the lips
- **tahu**, staring wildly and distorting the face
- **pōtētē**, a grimace.[17]

In an interview with Arapeta Awatere, Mervyn McLean was told that the term pōtētē:

. . . is used in Tūhoe and Ngāti Porou tribal areas not for haka leaders, but for the male tekoteko (clown) who taunts the enemy by spitting, sticking out his tongue, showing them his posterior and so on.[18]

Training for the pūkana could be arduous. Rangi Motu was chosen as a young girl to perform at the 1934 celebrations at Waitangi. Her training had started when she was very young:

My aunt taught me to cast my eyes down to the side, to look at a tin can which she had placed on the ground at an angle forward of where I stood, all the while keeping my head straight and forwards, just moving my eyes on their own. At each practice the can was moved along the ground closer and closer to my feet.

I was still to keep my head erect while looking at the object on the ground. It was only after long practice sessions that this was really mastered.[19]

In haka, the whole body is used to enhance the dance. Contorting the face, and using eyes and tongue allow the performer to reinforce the meaning and emphasise the force of the words used.

Traditional warrior performing haka with fierce facial expressions.

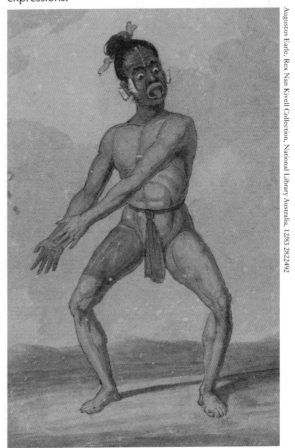

3 The tradition of haka

Haka — the rituals of encounter

Abel Tasman and James Cook, a Dutchman and an Englishman, were the first European explorers to observe Māori and report on their cultural practices. The first contacts between the great European nations and Māori were characterised by miscommunication and misunderstandings. As a consequence a number of these early encounters led to violence and deaths.

Abel Tasman

Abel Tasman was the first European explorer to record his interactions with Māori. Tasman, aboard his flagship the *Heemskerck*, accompanied by the smaller ship *Zeehaen*, sailed into Taitapu (Golden Bay) at the northern tip of the South Island late on the afternoon of 18 December 1642, having sailed up the country's west coast. Their arrival sparked immediate interest from the local people, thought to be members of Ngāti Tūmatakōkiri.

Ngāti Tūmatakōkiri very quickly sent out a reconnaissance party to investigate the ships. Anne Salmond, in her book *Two Worlds*, suggests that Ngāti Tūmatakōkiri would have been trying to understand what these strange ships were and would probably have chosen only the bravest warriors of the tribe to investigate.[1] The Dutch crew reported that the visitors seemed to be shouting and blowing trumpets. The crew responded and shot a cannon into the dark, which apparently incensed the Ngāti Tūmatakōkiri reconnaissance party.

The next day, several waka put to sea to further investigate the visitors. The Dutch crew reported that an old man in one of the waka shouted out in a rough voice. Salmond observes that this

> . . . *was probably a haka (war chant) provoked by the exchange of ritual challenges the night before. The Dutch completely misunderstood these signals, however.*[2]

It is probable at this stage that the Ngāti Tūmatakōkiri would have been planning to redress the insult offered them by the Dutch in refusing to respond to their challenge. As we shall

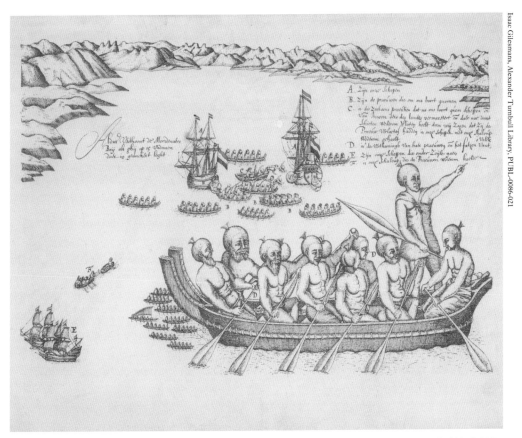

Isaac Gilsemans, Alexander Turnbull Library, PUBL-0086-021

First contact and haka challenge to Abel Tasman, performed in waka by Ngāti Tūmatakōkiri, 1642.

see later in this chapter, the rituals associated with encounters between two parties are prescribed by strict action and response drills. Lack of observance of these drills would be considered a serious breach of protocol, leading to retribution.

The Dutch, although not fully aware of what was happening, were prepared for action and they sent a small boat from the *Heemskerck* to warn the crew of the smaller ship to be on their guard. This boat was intercepted and rammed by Ngāti Tūmatakōkiri warriors and three Dutch crewmen were killed. The Dutch, enraged by this event, tried to retaliate using their cannons. However, the choppy sea conditions made it difficult for the shots to have any great effect. The Dutch soon left the area in disgust. Tasman named the bay Murderers' Bay after the incident, a name that signalled to the rest of the 'civilised' world that the natives they had come across were ferocious savages and should be avoided at all costs. The Dutch also christened the country after the Netherlands province of Zeeland.

James Cook

It was another 127 years before the next Europeans visited Aotearoa. Lieutenant James Cook arrived in early October 1769. Jean-François Marie de Surville, the French explorer, arrived in December of the same year, but he and Cook were unaware of each other's presence.

On the evening of 8 October 1769, Cook, aboard his ship *Endeavour*, hove to off Tūranganui-a-Kiwa, the traditional name for the site where Gisborne city now stands. The first casualty of this encounter between Māori and European occurred soon after a small English reconnaissance party had landed and was threatened by four warriors armed with long spears. Muskets fired into the air failed to deter the Māori as they advanced towards the landing party. Eventually the coxswain had to shoot one of the warriors. According to Salmond: '. . . this meeting was probably intended to be a ritual challenge rather than an ambush'.[3] Clearly the British did not know this and their reactions were swift and retaliatory.

The next day, 9 October, another party from the *Endeavour* attempted to land. A group of between 50 and 100 Māori had gathered. When Cook and his party called out to the Māori in Tahitian (Cook had brought from Tahiti a man called Tupaea to assist in communicating with Māori), the warriors reacted by rising fully armed, either with fighting spears or hand clubs.

According to an eyewitness, they began a war dance:

They seemed formed in ranks, each man jump'd with a swinging motion at the same instant of time to the right and left alternately accommodating a war song in very just time to each motion; their lances were at the same time elevated a considerable height above their heads.[4]

The observer noted that the warriors' tongues lolled out, their eyes were twisted up until the whites showed and their voices were hoarse and strong, calculated to

. . . Chear Each Other and Intimidate their Enemies, and may be call'd perhaps with propriety A Dancing War Song.[5]

Thus, for the first time in recorded history, Europeans were introduced to the full fury of a haka peruperu, performed by a group of warriors as a challenge to the visitors.

Sydney Parkinson's sketch 'New Zealand War Canoe Bidding Defiance to the Ship' shows how local groups greeted the *Endeavour*.

The haka was not restricted to being performed on land; it could also be performed vigorously in waka. The *Endeavour*'s surgeon, William Monkhouse, described an incident when the ship was anchored off Ahuriri (the present-day city of Napier). A number of waka rowed out to the *Endeavour* with the apparent intention of attacking her. In spite of a warning cannon shot fired across the bows of the waka, the Māori continued to chase the ship and eventually seven waka with about 160 warriors congregated at the stern of the *Endeavour*. The Māori performed their haka, accompanying their chants with a beating of their paddles on the cross-pieces of their waka:

> *A Man in the headmost Canoe at the same time, standing erect, Shouldered, poized and brandished his paddle with the true spirit of a Veteran. In some of his gesticulations great savageness was expressed — in bending forward, throwing his Arms behind him, elevating his head, staring wildly upwards, and thrusting his tongue forward, he exhibited a figure very like that expressed in the heads of their Canoes. . . . We commended the performance and they obliged us with a repetition of it.[6]*

In another encounter Cook's botanist Joseph Banks described how the warriors used their weapons and voices to complement the imagery of ferocity:

> *During this time they brandish their spears hack the air with their patoopatoos [short clubs] and shake their darts [short spears] as if they meant every moment to begin the attack, singing all the time in a wild but not disagreeable manner and ending every strain with a loud and deep fetchd sigh in which they all join in concert. The whole is accompanied by strokes struck against the sides of the Boats &c with their feet, Paddles and arms, the whole in such excellent time that tho the crews of several Canoes join in concert you rarely or never hear a single stroke wrongly placd.[7]*

Banks also described how the limbs and facial expressions were projected and contorted to create an image of ferocity and threat:

The War Song and dance consists of Various contortions of the limbs during which the tongue is frequently thrust out incredibly far and orbits of the eyes enlargd so much that a circle of white is distinctly seen round the Iris: in short, nothing is omittd which can render a human shape frightful and deformd, which I suppose they think terrible.[8]

Eighteenth- and nineteenth-century artists and haka

Several early artists succeeded in capturing some of the essence of the haka. A work by Sydney Parkinson, artist to Cook's 1769 expedition, perhaps best reflects the spontaneity of the haka carried out by warriors in a waka. His sketch shows a wide range of warrior postures. It is more than likely that in reality there would not have been so many chiefs standing up and leading the haka. Nevertheless, the sketch does give an impression of the ferocity one would have expected.

A painting by Louis Auguste de Sainson shows a haka being performed on board the *Astrolabe*, which visited Aotearoa New Zealand in 1827. Sainson's written description also captures the essential ingredients of the haka sequence in a graphic manner. He starts with the preparatory actions of summoning the troops:

One of them gave the recognised signal, and on the instant all his companions ran up taking their places in a single line beside him . . . They gave a prelude to their song by stamping their feet one after the other in perfect time and at the same time striking the top of their thighs with the palm of their hand.[9]

Louis Auguste de Sainson, Alexander Turnbull Library, B-052-

Haka performed by women and men on board the *Astrolabe* in Tasman Bay, early nineteenth century.

The expressions and postures make the haka unique and give it the air of threat and aggression:

> *Little by little their bodies are thrown back, their knees strike together, look like convulsions;*
> *their eyes turn up, so that with horrible effect, their pupils are absolutely hidden under*
> *the eyelids, while at the same time they twist their hands with outspread fingers rapidly*
> *before their faces.*[10]

The haka proper now begins and the sounds that issue forth from the mouths of the performers match the facial contortions and the eye movements as well as the protruding tongue gestures:

> *Now is the time when this strange melody takes on a character that no words can describe,*
> *but which fills the whole body with involuntary tremors. Only by hearing it can anyone*
> *form an idea of this incredible crescendo, in which each one of the actors appeared to us*
> *to be possessed by an evil spirit; and yet what sublime and terrible effects are produced*
> *by this savage music!*[11]

As the haka comes to an end and the wild expressions and coordinated chants begin to subside the performers almost retreat within themselves:

> *When by a final effort, the delirium of howls and contortions is borne to a climax, suddenly*
> *the whole group utters a deep moan and the singers, now overcome by fatigue, all let*
> *their hands drop at the same moment back on their thighs, then breaking the line they*
> *made, they seek the few moments rest which they desperately need.*[12]

Nineteenth-century observations

The interactions between Māori and the rapidly growing British population throughout the nineteenth century very much reflected the observations of the first European explorers. There was inevitably a sense of awe and at times bemusement at the haka being performed. It is not hard to imagine the shock felt by Europeans when observing the contortion of the facial features, especially the rolling of the eyes and the extraordinary protrusion of the tongue, coupled with the movement of feet and hands as well as weapons.

The early missionaries saw the haka from another perspective. They viewed haka as an essential and therefore threatening ingredient in the warlike ethos of the heathen warrior chiefs, which would hamper the missionaries' efforts to convert the chiefs and their followers. Henry Williams, local head of the Church Missionary Society, was at the forefront of missionary activities in Aotearoa New Zealand in the period between 1823 and 1840. Part of his campaign to bring Christianity to the country was to insist on Māori giving up their dances. Williams said:

> *I feel it necessary to prohibit all the old [Māori] customs, their dances, singing, and*
> *tattooing, their general domestic disorders. In Auckland the people are fond of assembling*
> *in large parties for the purpose of exhibiting their horrible dances.*[13]

As a means of communication and an integral part of various ceremonies, the haka was often misunderstood by Europeans. Throughout the latter part of the eighteenth and for at least half the nineteenth century it was misconstrued as a symbol of defiance at a time when Māori had little need to fear anyone.

Charles Emilius Gold, Alexander Turnbull Library, B-103-020

Women and men in haka, as depicted by Major Charles Gold.

The tradition of challenge and response

Since pre-European times the haka has been used as a part of the formal process when two parties come together. In earlier times, even when the purpose of the meeting was purportedly a peaceful one, it was still necessary to remain on guard in case one or the other party decided to use the opportunity to take advantage of the lack of preparedness of the other to attack and kill. Māori traditional history is redolent with examples of meetings with 'peaceful' intent being turned into violent attack.

The meeting of two parties of warriors was conducted according to certain rituals of encounter. The two parties followed well-understood rules of behaviour. As observed by Anne Salmond, in her ground-breaking book *Hui*:

> *In earlier times when warfare was endemic and strangers were probably enemies, these rituals were used as a finely balanced mechanism to manage encounters in peace . . . Even then they were not always successful, because between traditional rivals tempers ran high, and an exchange of insults or some unwitting offence could spark off hostilities on the spot.*[14]

The artist Augustus Earle observed the confrontation of two parties, which as Jennifer Shennan rightly observed was authentic and not arranged as a performance for him. Earle noted that:

40

As the opposite party landed, ours all crouched on the ground, their eyes fixed on the visitors, and perfectly silent . . . When they came very near, they suddenly stopped. Our party continued still mute, with their firelocks poised ready for use. For the space of a few minutes all was still, each party glaring fiercely at the other; and they certainly formed one of the most beautiful and extraordinary pictures I have ever beheld . . . The stillness of this extraordinary scene did not last long. The Narpooes [Ngāpuhi] commenced a noisy and discordant song and dance, yelling, jumping, and making the most hideous faces. This was soon answered by a loud shout from our party, who endeavoured to outdo the Narpooes in making horrible distortions of their own of their countenances: then succeeded another dance from our visitors: after which our friends made a rush, and in a sort of rough joke set them running. Then all joined in a pell-mell sort of encounter, in which numerous hard blows were given and received; then all the party fired their pieces in the air, and the ceremony of landing was thus deemed complete. They then approached each other, and began rubbing noses; and those who were particular friends cried and lamented over each other.[15]

Two parties meet

Elsdon Best described the process that occurred when two parties engaged on the marae. The tangata whenua or hosts assemble in columns on the courtyard. They all kneel on their left knee and hold their weapons with both hands. The approaching ope or travelling group slowly advances in columns towards the courtyard in silence. The group's leading chiefs and warriors are deployed to the front.

The challenge

When the ope nears the kneeling tangata whenua a challenger emerges from the silent ranks of the tangata whenua. He is selected for his appearance and bearing. He advances towards the approaching visitors with a light mānuka (wooden) spear and, after throwing it at them, turns and rapidly withdraws into the ranks of the tangata whenua.

A second warrior emerges from the kneeling ranks and approaches the nearing visitor party and also hurls his light spear at them and withdraws into the security of the assembled

Joseph Jenner Merrett, Alexander Turnbull Library, E-216-f-119

Traditional pōwhiri or ritual of encounter between two parties, Tauranga, early 1840s.

ranks of the kneeling tangata whenua. On both occasions the visitors ignore these challenges and steadily advance towards the courtyard.

Finally a third warrior emerges from the ranks of the tangata whenua. He has been chosen for his agility, speed and prowess. He advances towards the visitors and as he does so he gesticulates and grunts, leaping from side to side. When he is about 30 metres from the visitors he throws his spear and immediately turns to sprint back to the tangata whenua.

Suddenly, as the third spear lands in front of them, the visitors take action. From among their ranks emerges one of their finest warriors, who has been chosen for fleetness of foot and for courage in hand-to-hand combat. His task is to run the third challenger down before he gets back to his side. If the pursuer catches the challenger then he can either strike the runner down or thrust his weapon between the challenger's legs and throw him to the ground. Equally the challenger can turn to face the pursuer and engage him in hand-to-hand combat or trip him up.

Neither warrior must look back towards his side during the engagement as this would be a bad omen. Likewise, when the challengers turn to withdraw to their side, they must turn right and run back to the right-hand side of the tangata whenua group. Should the challenger reach the safety of his side the pursuer halts and kneels just short of the tangata whenua.

Meanwhile members of the visiting party have broken into a trot, taking short steps and uttering guttural sounds as they advance. When they reach the kneeling pursuer they halt.

The hosts then erupt into action on the call of one of their leaders. They rise and begin to advance to the right in the same short-stepping manner as the visitors. The two columns then pass each other

> *. . . in parallel lines with the same tramping tread, giving vent to the same weird cries. Their eyes stare wildly, their muscles are quivering, their actions and appearance denote excitement and defiance.*[16]

The response

When the tangata whenua reach the area where the third spear was thrown they turn to the right and trot back to where they have come from. The visitors also wheel to their right and withdraw. Again they pass each other

> *. . . in the same parallel manner, quivering with excitement, and half suppressed energy of voice and muscle, [while] the stamping of hundreds of bare feet upon the earth drones upon the ear.*[17]

On reaching their original positions there is a hushed pause. The silence is shattered by the leader of the tangata whenua springing to his feet and crying out for the warriors to rise. As one man, they arise and begin the haka peruperu, clutching their musket barrels with their right hands, the butts uppermost. The dance is indeed spectacular, as has been reported by those who were fortunate to observe such a sight. The visitors reciprocate and the noise, the ferocity and the competition all combine to create a truly fearful and spirited occasion.

After the haka peruperu, there is speech-making and then the parties come together to press noses in the hongi which concludes the event. This is usually followed by the tangata whenua providing food for the visitors.

Challenge and response

Challenge

1. The visiting ope advances towards the tangata whenua.

2. The tangata whenua group, kneeling in columns facing the advancing visitors, deploy three challengers. One by one, the challengers advance towards the visitors and throw light mānuka spears before sprinting back to their side.

3. The visiting group ignores the first two challengers and then chases the third.

Response

4. The tangata whenua group trots out to where the third spear was thrown. The group passes the visitors and then wheels and heads back to its original position and kneels facing the visitors.

5. The visiting group turns and trots back to its original position where the third spear was thrown. Once there, every man turns and kneels on his left knee, his right foot on the ground, his right hand grasping his weapon.

Haka peruperu and speeches

6. The tangata whenua group perform a haka peruperu.
7. The visiting group squat and observe the haka peruperu and then respond with their own haka.
8. The tangata whenua begin their speeches and the visitors respond.
9. After the speeches the parties move together to hongi.

1-2

3-4

5-7

8-9

The modern ritual of encounter

The elaborate form of the traditional ritual of encounter is not often seen these days. However, the principles that underlie the rituals are still used today in a modified form. For example, manuhiri or visitors will gather at the entrance to a marae. They will then be welcomed onto the marae by the tangata whenua, who will use a variety of mechanisms the most common of which is the karanga, or 'call', by an older woman of the marae. The karanga is a greeting that acknowledges the visitors, pays tribute to the departed and formally begins the process of the rituals of encounter. Because of the potential in traditional times for a kaikaranga (the caller) to be exposed to danger (and the vital importance to the tribe of protecting women who could bear children), this task fell to the older women of the marae who were past childbearing years.

From time to time, depending on the status of the visitors, a wero (challenge) may be offered prior to the karanga.

The visitors will then move onto the marae and may respond with their own karanga as they do so. The use of the haka is commonly used in a number of tribal areas as part of the welcoming ceremonies. It is generally used on important occasions for senior visiting dignitaries. On these occasions, the tangata whenua may send out up to three challengers, who, instead of throwing spears as in traditional times, will lay a small carved mānuka stick or small branch on the marae. This is picked up by the visitors as they advance and is an acknowledgement that the visiting party comes in peace.

Once the visitors have been seated on the marae, the tangata whenua begin the speeches. In some tribal areas, the tangata whenua all speak and then the manuhiri begin their speeches. In other areas, it is usual for speakers to alternate. Two of the tribal confederations I belong to adopt completely different approaches.

In Te Arawa it is customary for the speakers to alternate. The purpose of this approach is that the tangata whenua always have the first and last speakers on every occasion and in this way the mauri or life force of the marae remains with them. On occasions when there are large contingents of visitors and just a small handful of tangata whenua speakers it is usual after the first speaker has spoken to invite the visitors to put up all their speakers. When they have concluded their speeches the tangata whenua speaker stands to end the speeches.

On my Mātaatua side we adopt a different approach. All of our speakers speak first. The opportunity is then provided for the visitors or manuhiri to speak. When their speakers have concluded we can either bring the mauri back to the tangata whenua by having someone stand and conclude, or we may move directly to inviting the manuhiri to come and hongi.

It is customary at the end of each speech for the support team to stand beside the speaker and sing a waiata. This is often referred to as the kīnaki, or relish. If the speech is good then it deserves a good song of support to complement it.

When speeches have been completed, the manuhiri are then invited to hongi with the tangata whenua. After this ritual of greeting it is usual for the manuhiri to be invited for a cup of tea. The taking of food is the final step in the process. The removal of any spiritual barriers has now been completed. This means that the visitors have now been embraced by the hosts and for the duration of their stay on the marae they are effectively treated as if they were tangata whenua.

It is bad manners to leave the marae without completing this last step.

'Ka Mate!' – the most famous haka of all

4

Below is a verse from the haka pōkeka 'Ka Mate!':

Ā, ka mate! Ka mate!	'Tis death! 'Tis death!
Ka ora! Ka ora!	'Tis life! 'Tis life!
Ka mate! Ka mate!	'Tis death! 'Tis death!
Ka ora! Ka ora!	'Tis life! 'Tis life!
Tēnei te tangata pūhuruhuru	Behold! There stands the hairy man
Nāna nei i tiki mai whakawhiti te rā!	Who will cause the sun to shine!
Ā, hupane!	One step upwards,
Ā, kaupane!	another step upwards!
Ā, hupane!	One step upwards,
Ā, kaupane!	another step upwards!
Whiti te rā!	The sun shines!

These few lines are part of the haka performed by the All Blacks and other sports teams. This haka has become the focus of national and international attention, and has become an icon for Aotearoa New Zealand. However, few Aotearoa New Zealanders who perform the haka these days, and few who observe it, realise the enormous significance of its words or know anything of its intriguing history.

The pursuit of the warrior chief Te Rauparaha

The haka 'Ka Mate!' was composed in the early nineteenth century by Te Rauparaha, the famous fighting chief of Ngāti Toa, when he was on the run from pursuing warriors. It tells the simple story of pursuit and escape, fear of capture and the exhilaration of ultimate survival.

> *Na, ko Te Rauparaha te tama a Werawera o Ngāti Toa rāua ko tana wahine tuarua a Parekōwhatu o Ngāti Raukawa.*[1]

As recorded in *Ngā Tāngata Taumata Rau 1769–1789*, we find that Te Rauparaha was born the son of a chief called Werawera and his second wife, Parekōwhatu. As a consequence, he was linked to Ngāti Toa and Ngāti Raukawa, both tribes of the Tainui confederation.

Te Rauparaha was born and raised in Kāwhia. Because of his exploits in war and his readiness to capitalise on opportunities presented, he was marked out for promotion through the ranks over more senior chiefs. When still a young man, he attended a meeting at which the paramount chief Hapekitūārangi, of Ngāti Raukawa, was discussing who was to succeed him. He had called his tribe together to choose his successor. After a day of speeches he put the question to the tribe: 'Who is there among you that can take my place and tread in my path when I am gone?' As the contending chiefs muttered among themselves, Te Rauparaha stepped forward and exclaimed: 'I can!'[2]

Everybody was surprised, including the old man. However, since no one else stepped

Te Rauparaha's fleet approaching Kaiapoi to wreak vengeance on Ngai Tahu.

forward to claim his mantle, the chief acknowledged Te Rauparaha as the successor. When the old chief died Te Rauparaha not only married his widow but he also visited other tribes to pay his respects and to let them know he was now the paramount chief. In the years immediately after assuming power, Te Rauparaha often came into conflict with other tribes, because of his fiery temperament and unwillingness to step back.

The incident that gave rise to the haka 'Ka Mate!' took place when Te Rauparaha was travelling to meet Te Heuheu, the paramount chief of Ngāti Tūwharetoa, to seek his support against those aiming to defeat him.

As he journeyed around Lake Taupō, he heard that a group of warriors from Ngāti Te Aho, a sub-tribe of Ngāti Tūwharetoa, were waiting to ambush him. This was because, some years earlier, Te Rauparaha had attacked and wiped out a section of the Ngāti Te Aho people.

Te Rauparaha, on hearing of their plans, avoided the ambush and hurriedly made his way to see Te Heuheu and seek his protection. Te Heuheu said he could not protect Te Rauparaha as long as a section of his tribe was hostile to him. However, he told Te Rauparaha that he could seek protection from a chief called Wharerangi, who lived at Lake Rotoaira, south of Lake Taupō.

When Te Rauparaha reached the lake, he found to his disappointment that the people of Rotoaira were not friendly to him. Their chief, Wharerangi, was also troubled by Te Rauparaha's presence. However, since his paramount chief, Te Heuheu, had sent Te Rauparaha to him for protection he felt obliged to help even if his natural instinct was not to do so.

The chief hid Te Rauparaha in a pit in the ground, which was used for storing kūmara, the sweet potato. As Te Rauparaha lay hidden in the pit his pursuers neared the village. The two chiefs who were leading the chase were Tauteka and Te Riupāwhara. They began to scour the area in an effort to find him.

As the pursuing warriors neared the village where Te Rauparaha was hiding, they chanted karakia or incantations to paralyse Te Rauparaha and to block off his escape routes to the south-west. Sitting in the darkness, Te Rauparaha began to feel the effects of the incantations.

In the meantime Wharerangi's wife, Te Rangikoaea, had seated herself astride the entrance to the storage pit so that her pubic region lay over the entrance to it. The chants and incantations were neutralised by the way in which Te Rangikoaea had positioned herself over the pit entrance. To understand the significance of her actions we need to go back to the beginning of time and deep into the heart of Māori mythology (see The power of female sexuality, page 48).

Te Rauparaha, the famous Ngāti Toa fighting chief and author of the 'Ka mate!' haka.

The power of female sexuality

Te Rauparaha's pursuers chanted karakia in order to paralyse him. These karakia were neutralised by Te Rangikoaea because of the way she had positioned her genital region over the entrance to the pit where Te Rauparaha lay hidden. The source of the powers of female genitalia is located in Māori myth.

Hinenuitepō

Tānemahuta created the first woman and named her Hineahuone. A daughter of their union was Hinetītama, who subsequently was taken by her father as his partner. When she discovered that her lover was also her father she felt ashamed and escaped to the underworld, where she hid from the gods and renamed herself Hinenuitepō.

Some time later the demi-god Māui, in pursuit of immortality, decided that he would conquer Hinenuitepō by entering her through her genital region, thus reinforcing the power of the gods. Māui ventured down into the underworld in search of Hinenuitepō. He found her asleep with her legs wide open. Māui turned himself into a tuatara, crawled between her legs and entered her body. Hinenuitepō awoke and crushed Māui in the process.

Thus was the immortality of the gods diminished and the separation between mortals and immortals created, along with the fashioning of the world of light and life, and the underworld of death. It is for this reason that the genital region of the female body has powers that can defeat a male and neutralise karakia.

Hongi Hika and Te Aokapurangi

We need not go far back in our recorded history to find a powerful example of the significance of female genitalia. In 1823 a northern army of Ngāpuhi and allies, under the command of the redoubtable warrior Hongi Hika, attacked Mokoia Island in the middle of Lake Rotorua.[3]

The purpose for the expedition was to avenge the killing a year earlier of a warrior called Te Paeoterangi, the nephew of Hongi Hika. Interestingly, the killing of a group of Ngāpuhi by the Tūhourangi and elements of the Ngāti Whakaue tribes of Te Arawa was said to have been manipulated by Te Rauparaha while he was in the area seeking allies to join him

Hinenuitepō, goddess of the underworld, whose spirit protected Te Rauparaha.

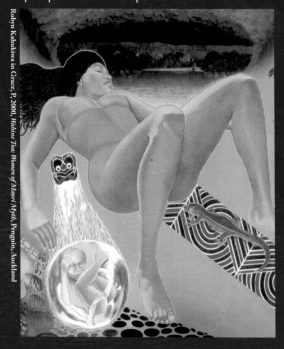

Robyn Kahukiwa in *Grace*, P. 2000, *Wahine Toa: Women of Māori Myth*, Penguin, Auckland

on Kāpiti Island in the Wellington region, which had become his stronghold.

Accompanying the war party from the north was a woman related to a number of tribes of Rotorua, especially to Tapuika and Ngāti Rangiwewehi. Her name was Te Aokapurangi, the wife of a senior Ngāpuhi chief. She had been captured in a Ngāpuhi raid of 1818 and taken back to the north, where she had married.

As the war party made its way down the North Island, Te Aokapurangi kept on asking Hongi Hika for forgiveness for her people. Hongi Hika agreed that they would not attack the Tapuika people but would save their energies for the killers of his nephew. At this stage he had not agreed to provide a blanket amnesty for her other relatives living in the Rotorua area.

When they neared Rotorua, and when Hongi lamented the fact that they would be slaying Te Aokapurangi's relatives, she again went to seek forgiveness for them. This was given and she went to the island to let her people know of the deal she had struck to save them.

The response from Hikairo, the leading chief of Ngāti Rangiwewehi, was a classical Māori response. He called out to her that they were indeed gratified by the Ngāpuhi gesture, however, he said: 'My word — take back to Ngāpuhi; the husband is embraced in the arms of the wife and cannot be withdrawn...'.[4] He could not leave his Te Arawa kin and chose instead to commit his whole tribe to their deaths if necessary.

When the attack finally got under way, Te Aokapurangi was in the vanguard as Hongi and his warriors landed on the island. During the battle the war chief relented and gave her permission to save her people as long as they '... were able to pass between her thighs'.[5]

During the cut and thrust of the battle she raced for the large meeting house called Tamatekapua and climbed up onto the roof. She sat astride the entrance to the meeting house and called for her relatives to come inside. Those that heeded the call passed between her legs and crammed into the house.

The pursuing warriors halted when they got to the door, firstly, because they knew she was married to one of the senior chiefs of Ngāpuhi, and secondly, and probably more importantly, they knew that in order to pursue the people inside they would need to walk between her legs and under her pubic region. This would have effectively robbed them of their mana (prestige) and accordingly they halted.

This was the reason that Hongi had added the stipulation requiring those who wanted to be spared to walk between her legs; he knew that few chiefs worth their salt would willingly give up their mana to save themselves.

The powerful Northern Chief, Hongi Hika.

Te Rauparaha escapes!

Meanwhile Te Rauparaha, although suffering the effects of the karakia, realised the incantations were being neutralised by Te Rangikoaea's genitals, and he imagined the incantations whirling around and being absorbed by Te Rangikoaea. He vented his feelings with the exclamation:

Āhaha!	Be prepared!
Kīkiki kākaka kau ana!	Let your valour arise! Let your temper rage!
Kei waniwania taku tara	We'll ward off the desecrating touch;
Kei tara wāhia, kei te rua i te kerokero!	We'll ward off the impious hand;
	We'll ne'er let the foe
	Outrage our cherished ones!
	We'll guard our women and our maidens;
	And be thou, O Leader, our boundary Pillar!

Although Te Rauparaha saw that the powers of the chieftainess were working, he realised it was essential to ensure that his protector was immune from any advances her husband made to her. He whispered:

He pounga rāhui te uira ka rarapa;	For ye all, I'll defy the lightning of the Heavens!
Ketekete kau ana tō peru kei riri	The foe, he will stand frustrated;
Mau au e koro e —	In his mad and impotent rage!
Hī! Hā!	Mine ears will then be spared
Ka wehi au ka matakana.	The maiden's despairing cry
	Will ye, O Sir, possess me?
Ko wai te tangata kia rere ure?	The thought it makes me quail!
Tirohanga ngā rua rerarera	Who in his manhood will stand affrighted;
Ngā rua kurī kaka nui i raro!	Or in his terror flee?
	For he will surely perish
	And in the refuse pit will lie
	As food for dogs to gnaw with relish![6]

As the pursuers neared, Te Rauparaha could hear the trample of their feet. Tauteka, one of the chiefs pursuing Te Rauparaha, questioned Wharerangi about Te Rauparaha's whereabouts. Beset by doubt and anxiety, Te Rauparaha muttered to himself:

Ka mate! Ka mate!	'Tis death! 'Tis death!

His fate hung in the balance as he lay in the darkness of the kūmara pit. He knew what was in store for him if they found him. When Wharerangi told Tauteka that Te Rauparaha had escaped to the Rangipō Plains, Te Rauparaha began to breathe a sigh of relief:

Ka ora! Ka ora!	'Tis life! 'Tis life!

He felt the lifting of fear and tensions and a sense of relief when he heard Wharerangi trying to send the pursuers off in another direction. However, his relief was short-lived as Tauteka doubted Wharerangi's word. Once more his thoughts turned to death:

| Ka mate! Ka mate! | 'Tis death! 'Tis death! |

Surely this time they would find him? Finally, though, Tauteka believed Wharerangi, and the warriors turned to leave the village. As his pursuers' footsteps receded, Te Rauparaha's thoughts turned again to life:

| Ka ora! Ka ora! | 'Tis life! 'Tis life! |

This time his hunters did not return. As he looked upwards and began to climb out of the pit his expression of exultation was palpable as he gave thanks to his saviour.

| Tēnei te tangata pūhuruhuru, | Behold! There stands the hairy man |
| nāna nei i tiki mai, whakawhiti te rā! | Who will cause the sun to shine! |

The commonly held view is that Te Rauparaha was paying tribute to the chief Wharerangi, who was said to have hairy legs. However, among Ngāti Toa there is another version, which on the face of it seems equally plausible. It is suggested that in fact Te Rauparaha was paying tribute to the chieftainess who sat astride the entrance to the pit. And far from being the man with the hairy legs, his saviour was the old woman sitting astride the entrance to the pit, with her pubic area exposed!

This latter version is supported by John Grace in his book *Tuwharetoa*.[7] According to Grace, as Te Rauparaha emerged from the entrance to the kūmara pit he went onto the courtyard of the village and before Wharerangi and Te Rangikoaea he performed his now famous haka.

It also makes greater sense when one understands the significance of the old woman's actions. In Māori tradition, for men, the female pubic region is as much a symbol of mystery and spiritualism as it is a potential means of removing their mana. That is also why today, when females stay overnight at a marae, they must avoid stepping over a sleeping man, lest they should diminish his mana. Finally, as he climbed out of the pit, Te Rauparaha called out:

Ā, hupane! Ā, kaupane!	One step upwards, another step upwards!
Ā, hupane! Ā, kaupane!	One step upwards, another step upwards!
Whiti te rā!	The sun shines!

His escape was complete.

'Ka Mate!' becomes part of history

Few tribes except Ngāti Toa perform the full haka, and the verse at the start of this chapter is the portion that has become most well known.

Some 30 years after the incident involving Te Rauparaha, the haka was used on

Motutere marae to celebrate the reconciliation of two chiefs of Tūwharetoa: Iwikau Te Heuheu and Te Kiekie. Interestingly, Te Kiekie was the son of Tauteka, the chief who had chased Te Rauparaha and had stood outside the kūmara pit questioning Wharerangi about Te Rauparaha's whereabouts! The reconciliation had been brought about by the Reverend TS Grace, who insisted on both chiefs making up and becoming allies again.

As John Grace described the occasion:

Grace then made them hongi in his presence and then, taking them outside before the assembled tribes, made them repeat the gesture. The tribes rose up under the leadership of their respective chiefs and thundered out the haka which Te Rauparaha had composed at Motuopuhi. The significance in this instance was that Grace, who had a beard, was the hairy man who was responsible for bringing peace into the camp and, as they put it, causing the sun to shine again and light up the gloomy realms of Ngati Tuwharetoa.[8]

Although the haka 'Ka Mate!' has become popularised in Aotearoa New Zealand, for the Ngāi Tahu tribe of the South Island the performance of 'Ka Mate!' is not an occasion for celebration. In the 1980s I was told of a university group from the North Island that had travelled down to the South Island as part of an inter-university exchange. They stayed overnight at a Ngāi Tahu marae and, because of the lateness of their arrival, were not formally received onto the marae until just on dusk. The tangata whenua welcomed the group, sang their waiata, and then allowed the manuhiri their chance to respond. One of the young northern visitors began his speech with the haka 'Ka Mate!'. He was surprised when none of his fellow visitors got up to join him. As soon as he began, all the Ngāi Tahu speakers stood up and said, 'E tau! E tau!' (Sit down! Sit down!) The visitor was put out by this hostile reception to the haka. He had obviously not been listening when the leader of his group had previously outlined why they were not to perform the haka 'Ka Mate!' on a Ngāi Tahu marae.

The significance of 'Ka Mate!' for Ngāi Tahu relates to a trip made by Te Rauparaha in 1830. He set out to exact revenge on an old foe, Te Maiharanui, a chief of northern Ngāi Tahu. Te Rauparaha enlisted the aid of Captain Stewart and his ship, the *Elizabeth*, to take him and 200 of his warriors to the South Island to help him conqueror his enemies.[9] On arriving off Akaroa, the *Elizabeth* anchored and gave the impression it was ready to trade. Meanwhile Te Rauparaha and his men remained hidden below decks.

Eventually Captain Stewart, having sent a number of messages, got Te Maiharanui and his young daughter on board. Te Maiharanui was seized by Te Rauparaha and was placed in chains. Over the next few days he captured the girl's mother Te Whē and other relatives as well. The parents, knowing what was in store for them, strangled their daughter.

After a week, Te Rauparaha returned to his North Island stronghold of Kāpiti Island (located off the coast north of Wellington) where he tortured the chief and his wife before killing them.

This incident left Ngāi Tahu outraged. Te Rauparaha made subsequent expeditions south and was eventually repelled.

If there is a moral to this story it is as old as time itself: look before you leap; or don't do a haka unless you fully understand it and its implications. It would be interesting to know how Ngāi Tahu feel about the All Blacks performing the haka 'Ka Mate!' at Jade Stadium in Christchurch before a rugby test match!

Cultural resurgence through haka and kapa haka

Inter-tribal rivalry has always been a feature of Māori tradition. In the pre-contact period the effects of inter-tribal warring were moderated by the use of traditional weaponry and the practice of utu (exacting revenge) to maintain equilibrium. Most battles did not rise above small-scale, symbolic skirmishes. With the introduction of muskets and other foreign weapons, however, this balanced rivalry was transformed into devastating slaughter in the 1820s and 1830s. These bloody encounters, known as the Musket Wars, changed the face of tribal relations in a way that still resonates today.

Clashes between tribes continued sporadically after the 1830s, but from 1840 onwards a new threat occupied Māori, as British attempts to wrest control of the land from Māori erupted into full-scale wars. The latter part of the nineteenth century was devastating for Māori, with bitterly fought conflicts with the British and subsequent land confiscations by the government. New legislation allowing private land sales resulted in the loss of prime Māori land, at the same time as increasing European immigration swamped Māori numerically. The effect of introduced diseases was also acute, and by 1900 the Māori population had dropped to an estimated 42,000. Māori continued to lose the struggle to hold on to their lands and witnessed the diminution of their culture.

It was against this backdrop that Māori began the new century, still determined to preserve their cultural traditions, to organise politically and develop new leaders, and to show pride in their tribes and traditions. Ironically the major catalysts for the resurgence of Māori regaining their cultural heritage were the tours by British royalty of Aotearoa New Zealand.

Royal visit 1901

Nineteen hundred and one was the year in which cultural competition among the tribes was launched on an unprecedented scale. Māori gathered in their thousands in Rotorua to celebrate the visit of the Duke and Duchess of Cornwall and York. It was only 20 years earlier that the pacifist revolt at Parihaka in Taranaki, led by the prophets Te Whiti-o-Rongomai and Tohu Kākahi, had fizzled out under the overwhelming threat of Pākehā soldiers and constabulary. Parihaka was almost the last flick of the tail of Māori resistance against the now dominant Pākehā culture, although it was not until another 15 years later, with the arrest of the Tūhoe prophet Rua Kenana in 1916, that the threat of civil unrest was finally removed.

William Henry Thomas Partington, Alexander Turnbull Library, G-3142-1/1

Haka party ready for action on the occasion of the Royal visit of the Duke and Duchess of Cornwall and York to Rotorua 1901.

Many of the spectators at the cultural displays and some of the leading chiefs who performed with their contingents, like Te Pōkiha Taranui (Major Fox) of Te Arawa, had fought in the land wars of the 1860s and 1870s. For many the wars, from which many of the dances and songs had sprung, were still relatively fresh in their minds. For the younger performers, just one generation removed from this time of war, it was still alive in the memories of the elders and the stories told at hui (gatherings). Thus fuelled with the stories of the recent past and still strong with the learned skills of the art of dance and song, the 1901 celebrations were bound to be a hugely exciting and entertaining time.

While there were no prisoners or bodies to be taken from the field of endeavour to signify a victory as in ancient times, nevertheless the tribes came from their villages imbued with the spirit of the challenge to represent their tribes to the best of their abilities at this massive event.

The royal visit came hard on the heels of the death of Queen Victoria, and so provided an opportunity to pay homage to the woman who had signed the Treaty of Waitangi along with their ancestors in 1840, some 61 years earlier, when only 21 years of age.

The event brought the tribes together in numbers that had rarely been seen before. It is likely that more than 10 per cent of the total Māori population gathered together to celebrate the arrival of royalty.

The summons to meet at Rotorua had been sent throughout the land three months ahead of time by the Minister of Native Affairs, himself a Māori, the Honourable James Carroll, or 'Timi Kara'.

The hosts for this vast occasion were Te Arawa. They prepared a party of 1200 performers for the occasion, under the stringent exhortation from tribal elders that they were not to betray the pride of the tribe. In other words, they had to ensure that they took every opportunity to show the other tribes as well as the visitors how good they were at performing haka.

Ngāpuhi, from the north, were returning to Rotorua in numbers for the first time since their raid in 1823, some 78 years earlier. While the event was held in a spirit of cooperation and hospitality for the overseas visitors, there would have been a few in Te Arawa plotting revenge — only this time, the utu would have to be exacted on the field of competition rather than the field of combat as in ancient times.

The combined tribes of the East Coast, Ngāti Porou and Ngāti Kahungunu, with their shared heritage, came to Rotorua with the reputation of being the foremost haka exponents and in the eyes of most other tribes were the tribe to beat.

The neighbouring Mātaatua confederation sent representatives of the tribes including Ngāi Te Rangi from Tauranga, Ngāti Awa from Whakatāne, Tūhoe from the forests of Te Urewera and Te Whakatōhea from the coastal plains. All were determined to pit themselves against some of the bigger tribes whose reputations were nationally acknowledged.

For two weeks before the arrival of the royal party the tribes rehearsed. From early dawn until late each night the parties practised under the guidance of their tohunga and chiefs. No detail was too small and rehearsals, when conducted publicly, were critically analysed by the scouts of the other contingents. This was a time of unprecedented unity among individual tribes as they strove to perfect their performance and their dances and songs.

This was time also for all the great chiefs to become actively involved. Senior members of the Executive Committee that planned the events of the 1901 hui were also actively involved with their tribes:

Te Heuheu could be seen at the head of Ngatituwharetoa; [Apirana] Ngata on the flanks of the deep ranks of Ngatiporou; and Heke, though not in costume, controlled the restless Ngapuhi. All the prominent men were seen marshalling their clans.[1]

Chief Marumaru from Wanganui, chairman of the organising committee, and the Minister of the Crown, Timi Kara, also headed their tribal delegations.

Meanwhile the tussle for the accolades continued throughout the days of the celebrations. The hosts, Te Arawa, led by Te Pōkiha Taranui, were determined to succeed as the best performing group. A reporter noted:

It is hard to state what was the characteristic of the admirable performance of these the tangata whenua, who had vowed not to suffer defeat in the friendly rivalry on their own marae. In the volume of sound produced they were first for theirs was the largest taua [group], and incessant practice had made their throats as of brass. They made a great impression. One picture lingered in the mind's eye for days afterwards: that of the venerable Pokiha Taranui . . . aged and dying, yet calling up his last reserve of energy — almost to the last flicker of life as it proved later on — to swing the big claymore, the sword of honour presented to him by the Queen, wildly before the wide front of his taua.[2]

The Ngāpuhi people were also very keen to make an impression. Their impatience almost boiled over as they took the centre stage and performed their ancient haka peruperu 'A kei te Wīwī, A kei te Wāwā:

They leaped from side to side with tumultuous energy, swinging their spears and shaking the ground with the thud of their feet as the ancient war cry of their race resounded, deep, peremptory, stirring.[3]

Thus were the tribes gathered together for the first of the great celebrations to welcome members of the royal family. The Duke and Duchess and the royal entourage left the celebrations sated with the extraordinary spectacles they had witnessed. Soldier members of the entourage likened the dying sighs of the haka to the heroic call of the legions of Rome as in ancient times they marched past their emperors, committing themselves to service to the empire.

Regaining cultural strength

In the early part of the twentieth century many tribes struggled to make headway at a time when population numbers were low and disease and deprivation were still prevalent. However, Māori gained a political voice with seats reserved for them in Parliament, and lobbied on issues that affected them. Members of the Young Māori Party sought improved health and education services for Māori communities.

Sir Āpirana Ngata (knighted in 1927 for his services to the Māori people) was the outstanding Māori leader of the twentieth century. Born in the latter half of the nineteenth century in the nurturing fold of the senior chieftainship lines of his tribe Ngāti Porou, he emerged out of the traditional schools of learning and began the pursuit of European knowledge that would see him catapulted to the most senior ranks of Aotearoa New Zealand society.

Ngāti Porou leader and politician Apirana Ngata leads his tribe in a haka at Waitangi in 1934.

His was a life of many firsts. Much of the responsibility for regrowing a vibrant population and for rebuilding successful tribal economic bases rested on his shoulders. He entered Parliament in 1906 and became Minister of Native Affairs in 1928. He based his recovery programme on the establishment of land development schemes and the reinvigoration of cultural strengths. Under his guidance land schemes, tribal development and cultural regrowth flourished. Sir Apirana's son Hēnare described his father's achievements in a letter he wrote to Eric Ramsden, who was preparing for publication a book entitled *Sir Apirana Ngata and Maori Culture*:

> *The encouragement of arts and crafts, culminating in a large number of Maori meeting houses all over the country, was merely another step on the social and cultural level, in preserving Maoritanga. . . . Haka and actions songs, and so on, have been encouraged with the same end in view: some times with an admixture of Pakeha flavour (as a concession to the times) but always retaining their distinctive essence. Through these things . . . a resurgence of pride has taken place, especially among a generation born to a modern environment. That pride has, however, been cultivated not as an instrument of arrogant nationalism but as a means of providing us with a foundation on which to build our self-respect.*[4]

Notwithstanding Ngata's Herculean efforts during which he personally visited and led many of the cultural projects, many tribes struggled to retain their cultural heritage. In 1934, in preparation for the celebrations to be held at Waitangi, Ngata was forced to send one of Ngāti Porou's pre-eminent haka specialists to the north to train and teach Ngāpuhi in the arts of the haka, as their knowledge base had deteriorated significantly.[5]

It was in this year also that Lady Bledisloe, wife of the Governor-General, presented the Te Rēhia trophy for competition among Māori groups and communities in song, dance and oratory.

At the outbreak of the Second World War there was a further upsurge in cultural activity as tribes reclaimed ancient haka and updated them as a tribute to their young men going off to war. When the 1940 celebrations were held at Waitangi, the 28th (Māori) Battalion provided a large contingent to take part in the celebrations. Their input was significant and marked another milestone in the tribes recovering their pride and their willingness to test themselves and their haka on high-profile public occasions.

Throughout this entire period Ngata's hand could be clearly seen. He was unremitting in his efforts and always took the opportunity to teach, to lead and to demonstrate. While in his 74th year and attending a Māori Anglican hui at Te Poho-o-Rāwiri marae in Gisborne, Ngata showed as always his inimitable style and commitment. The hui had ended earlier than planned and people were enjoying a cup of tea and chatting when a group of young people started to entertain the hui. They sang Ngata's own composition 'He Putiputi Pai'.

Ngata, pipe in hand — as usual it was unlit — sipped his tea, smiling enigmatically. At last he could remain silent no longer. Casting aside his coat, he joined the juveniles. Then, he put the rangatahi through their paces, demonstrating gesture by gesture, how the song should be sung. The old man then led them in the rousing Ngāti Porou haka 'Rūaumoko'.[6]

During the 1950s and early 1960s cultural competitions were also a major part of the annual church gatherings. Thousands of Māori gathered for religious observances, to play sport and to dance, sing and haka. The Māori wing of the Catholic Church held its annual celebrations, Hui Aranga, in Easter of each year and the Anglicans held their Hui Tōpū each May.

From the 1960s onwards there has been increasing Māori political activism, along with a great revival in Māori language, arts and culture.

A solitary woman leads the haka party at Rotorua, 1901.

More royal visits — presenting Māori culture

Over the past 100 years Māori have seldom risen to the challenge of competing against each other in song and dance as they have on the occasion of the visits of members of the British royal family. While in recent years the glamour and importance of royal visits have somewhat diminished, there still remains in the minds of those who have taken part in these events a sense of pride and achievement and a satisfaction at having pitted their skills against the best.

In 1901 Māori tribes gathered at Rotorua, in what was a huge event for the time, to celebrate the visit of the Duke and Duchess of Cornwall and York. The occasion provided an opportunity to showcase the haka talents of each tribe and compete with old foes, this time on the stage rather than the battlefield.

Royal visits provided a benchmark for public performances of haka. In 1920 another royal visitor, the Duke of Windsor, also visited Rotorua. Fifty-two years after the 1901 celebrations, the tribes gathered again at Rotorua. This time the occasion was to acknowledge the death of King George VI and greet his successor.

In 1953, Queen Elizabeth II, the great-great-granddaughter of Queen Victoria, came to Rotorua as part of her royal tour. Thousands turned out for her visit and the haka parties were again an essential element of the pomp and pageantry of the day. Hundreds of primary school children lined the royal party's route through the town.

I was 10 years of age at the time and I can recall getting ready early that morning at the Rotoiti Primary School to travel by bus to the occasion. It was a long and hot day for us. I can remember the huge crowds, the cheering, being thirsty and catching a mere glimpse of the royal cavalcade as it swept past us. Nevertheless it was an unforgettable occasion, made more impressive by the assembled tribes and their haka.

A haka party in action during the Duke of Windsor's tour to Rotorua in 1920.

Takitimu welcomes Queen Elizabeth II in 1986

When the Queen visited Aotearoa New Zealand in 1986 it was decided that a national Māori welcome would be extended to her at Nelson Park, Hastings, on 25 February 1986. The programme for the visit allowed Ngāti Kahungunu to showcase its traditional action songs and haka. It also provided an opportunity for invited tribes and groups to perform for the nation.

The first item to be performed was a haka tūtūngārahu performed by the hosts Ngāti Kahungunu:[7]

He taua, he taua	The party approaches — the visitors appear before us!
I a hei!	Yes, yes
He taua, he taua	The party approaches — they come in force!
I a hei!	Yes, yes
Whakarite, whakarite	Then make ready, be ready!
A kia rite	Yes to be ready!
Kī mai ngā atua	The gods of the night
O te pō	Declared to all
Ka tuhi, ka rapa, ka uira	The sky reddens lightning flashes and vents its wrath
Ka tō te māhū	Everywhere it abates not
Ki okioki e	It rests not
Tōia te waka	Let the canoe be moved on
Pōuri, pōuri	Now it is dark
Pōtango, pōtango	So very dark!
Whākere, whākere rā	Utterly dark!
I mau ai te tīeke he matarau	Wherefore is worn the cloak
Haere, haere ki te wīwī	The cloak is worn
Haere, haere ki te wāwā	Move on in caution
Kia whakamau ai	Move on in anxiety
Kia tīna, tīna	Move on with faith
Hui ē tāiki ē	United
Tūtūngārahu	Behold it is done
Makamaka whana	Now dance in readiness for battle
Ngā āhei hei	Yes the war dance
Whakarehu, whitiapu	Your weapons at attention
Te ōtane	The forward thrust — the downward blow
Te uri o Kahungunu	The horizontal crossguard position
Kia rite, kia rite	For we descend from Kahungunu himself

Te whana kaitangata e	Now ready for battle!
Pakanga Parekura	Yes. The charge of annihilation!
Hei, hei, hei	To battle! To battle!
Ngau ki te oneone	We strike
Ngau ki te paruparu	That one bites the earth
He taua	That one eats filth
He taua toto	We are a war party
Whakarehu	A war party without compromise
Aa!	The final thrust
	It is done.

This haka was followed by two haka pōwhiri. The first of these is a welcome from the peoples of the Takitimu waka, the waka of Ngāti Kahungunu. The second is a haka pōwhiri (whakawhiti) 'Tōia Mai'. This is a traditional haka that draws the visitors forward onto the marae. The haka is about dragging a waka from its moorings to a safe place on land.

A tōia mai	Now draw hither
Te waka	The canoe (of her Majesty Queen Elizabeth II)
Ki te urunga	Up onto the pillow
Te waka	The canoe
Ki te moenga	To the resting place
Te waka	The canoe
Ki te takotoranga	To the place of rest
Takoto ai	To be installed
Te waka.	The canoe.

Speeches of welcome followed. The Minister of Māori Affairs, the Hon Koro Wetere, started proceedings. He was followed by Sir James Henare from the North. Sir James was followed by Sir Hepi Te Heuheu, the paramount chief of Ngāti Tūwharetoa. Sir Hēnare Ngata spoke for Ngāti Porou and Joe Karetai spoke for Ngāi Tahu. After each speaker an item was performed. In Sir Hepi's case his haka group performed the Wairangi haka (see page 20).

Daily Telegraph

Ngāti Kahungunu warriors lead haka pōwhiri for Queen Elizabeth II at Hastings, 1986.

6 Tribal haka composers

Some tribes are renowned for particular activities or traits. The Te Arawa tribe in the Bay of Plenty have always been associated with tourism and have carved out an enduring reputation for being entertainers, since the latter part of the nineteenth century.

The Mātaatua confederation of tribes have always been associated with the waiata of Te Kooti Rikirangi, the warrior prophet. Ngāpuhi in the north, while retaining a strong language base, has as a consequence of early and sustained interaction with missionaries in the nineteenth century lost many of its traditional haka and waiata.

All tribes have had composers and tohunga in their histories renowned for their waiata and haka.

Ngāti Porou

Some of the most dynamic and well-known haka and kapa haka items have come and continue to come from the East Coast. For each generation over the past 100 years the Ngāti Porou people have produced composers and compositions that have arguably placed them at the apex of haka and kapa haka in Aotearoa.

It is interesting to observe that notwithstanding this deep reservoir of cultural talent over the years Ngāti Porou teams have not until recently actively taken part in kapa haka competitions. Their unique laid-back style of performance, reflective of another age, is in direct contrast to the urgency and the frenetically zealous performance of many other tribes.

Ngāti Porou is one of the few tribes in Aotearoa that is proudly matrilineal. The role of women in the tribal histories is dominant and is reflected in many of the wharenui (meeting houses) being named after female ancestors. In contrast, most other tribes are patrilineal and their wharenui are largely named after male ancestors. It is perhaps for this reason that Ngāti Porou women play a significant role in the composition and performance of haka.

Tuta Nihoniho — 'Te Kiri Ngutu'

Tuta Nihoniho was born in 1850 at Whareponga on the East Coast. He was part of the Ngāti Porou contingent under the command of Major Rōpata Wahawaha which fought against Pai Marire rebels on the East Coast during the latter parts of the land wars. Notwithstanding his support for the Crown he led the protests against what he and his fellow Ngāti Porou chiefs thought were unfair laws and regulations. It was this innate sense of right and wrong that led him to modify the ancient haka 'Te Kiri Ngutu'.

This famous Ngāti Porou haka has been handed down through the generations. According to the Rev Tipi Kaa the following commentary on the haka was given to him by Sir Āpirana Ngata:

This Composition has come down the generations and had its greatest revival with topical adaptations in 1888, when the Porourangi meeting house was formally opened. Led by the late Tuta Nihoniho, a noted chief of the Hikurangi sub-tribes, a section of Ngati Porou registered their protest against the rating of their lands and the taxation of articles of every-day consumption, specifying the 'pua torori' or the tobacco plant. It was revived again at the Waitangi celebrations in 1934 and was adopted by the men of the 9th and 10th Maori Reinforcements as the 'piece de resistance' of the recent celebration of the opening of Tamatekapua at Rotorua. Its main theme is not outdated, the complementary, yet seemingly,

Tuta Nihoniho of Hikurangi, Ngāti Porou: nineteenth century chief, soldier and composer of the anti-government haka 'Te Kiri Ngutu'.

Jane McDonald, Museum of New Zealand Te Papa Tongarewa

contradictory features of civilisation with the still novel but bitter pill of taxation. In the circumstances the vigour of the recitative and concomitant actions may be appreciated.[1]

The Rev Kaa himself observed that the haka 'Te Kiri Ngutu' is performed by Ngāti Porou on important occasions. He suggests that while the text can be seen as being hostile to Pākehā Aotearoa New Zealanders, its contemporary use can be seen as an act of 'respectful greeting'. More to the point it demonstrates the 'proud and defiant spirit of Ngāti Porou'.

Set out below is the first part of the haka: the whakaara or the introductory verse. This part of the haka focuses on the Parliament and its laws and the imposition of rates and taxation. Later in the haka there is an attack on Pākehā purchase of Māori land, especially in the Gisborne area, an area to which Tuta Nihoniho was affiliated.

Te Kiri Ngutu — whakaara (the awakening)

Kaea:	Ponga ra! Ponga ra!	Leader:	The shadows fall! The shadows fall!
Katoa:	Ka tataki mai te	Chorus:	The House which makes
	Whare o ngā ture!		the laws is chattering
	Ka whiria te Māori! Ka whiria!		And the Māori will be plaited as a rope
	Ngau nei ōna reiti (E)		Its rates and its
	ngau nei ōna tāke!		taxes are biting!
	Ahaha! Tē taea te ueue!		Ahaha! Its teeth cannot be withdrawn!
	I auē! Hā!		Alas!
Kaea:	Patua i te whenua	Leader:	The land will be destroyed!
Katoa:	Hei!	Chorus:	Hei!
Kaea:	Whakataua i ngā ture!	Leader:	The laws are spread-eagled over it!
Katoa:	Hei!	Chorus:	Hei!
Kaea:	Ahaha!	Leader:	Ahaha!
Katoa:	Nā ngā mema rā te kōhuru	Chorus:	The members have done this black deed,
	Nā te Kāwana te kōheriheri!		And the rulers have conspired in the evil;
	Ka raruraru ngā ture!		The laws of the land are confused,
	Ka raparapa ki te		For even the tobacco leaf
	pua tōrori! I auē!		is singled out! Alas!

Lieutenant-Colonel Arapeta Awatere

If Tuta Nihoniho and Sir Apirana Ngata were the cultural bridges between the nineteenth and twentieth centuries in respect of haka and kapa haka compositions and knowledge then an outstanding master of the twentieth century was Arapeta (Pita) Awatere.

Like Nihoniho and Ngata, Awatere was another product of classical traditional training. His upbringing was focused on the transmission of traditional knowledge from his elders. He also displayed a musical and poetic ability in both English and his native Māori. He rose through the ranks in the Second World War to eventually lead the 28th (Māori) Battalion. He was an eccentric warrior, whose habit of conducting his own reconnaissance patrols in no-man's-land was most disconcerting to his commanders, let alone his own troops. Awatere applied his acutely tuned mind to whatever endeavour he tackled. His demand for the utmost

discipline and focus of his troops carried over into his role as a welfare officer working for the Department of Māori Affairs after the war. He took every opportunity to train and practise with kapa haka groups and loved performing the haka, especially the classic Ngāti Porou haka he knew as a child and young man growing up.

Pita Awatere's relentless pursuit of excellence and his unrelenting style of training were exemplified when he trained a group of about 60 young people from Waitara. The occasion was a visit on 8 August 1954 by the Governor-General Sir Willoughby Norrie to Waitara to honour the death of Sir Peter Buck (Te Rangi Hiroa).

Sir Peter had died some three years earlier and his ashes had been borne from Honolulu by the Minister of Māori Affairs the Hon EB Corbett. Awatere imposed a ruthless training regime from 8pm until midnight. A *Te Ao Hou* reporter said he was assured by Awatere that the methods being used to train the youth were traditional. The reporter observed that this seemed to consist in:

> *. . . exciting in the group the emotion appropriate to the dance, and then leaving the members free to express this emotion in their own way. Technique is not forgotten. In the haka, said the tutor, young people should always keep their feet apart. Older ones, he inferred, could introduce any appropriate variations they fancied. And, 'keep your eyes above your audience all the time until you are old enough to look at them'. For Maori youth is shy and to display the full excitement of the haka takes boldness . . . or lack of self-consciousness. Training in reciting the words precedes the teaching of the actions. Points of elocution are vigorously stressed — 'Pronounce the last syllable of a word, open your mouth,' — and the teacher prances in front of his group in a fierce haka with his finger pointing at his wide open mouth. He inspires through example; performing continually at his best he gives out his own artistry and his stirring dance movements transfer his own animation to the group.[2]*

The relentless nature of Awatere's training approach was best reflected in the concern expressed by local women that there should be a break for a cup of tea. Awatere scornfully rejected such an idea. The *Te Ao Hou* reporter captured his views:

> *These frequent meals were a European idea that only softened and dissipated the people. They broke down concentration. The rehearsal went on without a murmur and strangely enough, the standard began to rise rapidly. The same girls who put on something a little mediocre early in the evening gave a finely disciplined performance, and now the teacher concentrated on their action song and the boys got a brief rest.[3]*

Lieutenant Colonel Arapeta Awatere: poet, musician, composer and war-time commander of the 28th (Maori) Battalion.

Women and haka

Traditional role of women in haka

The role of women is an interesting aspect of the performance of the haka. Generally, there is little contemporary written material on the topic. However, in tribes where women have played a much greater role in the tribe's history and assume a greater role in the development of its culture, we can find examples of women playing a significant, and sometimes dominant, role.

Te Hāmana Mahuika, a Ngāti Porou expert on the haka, sets out a number of rules to be applied to men and women involved in the haka. The man is responsible for the aggression, the provocation and the overt expressions associated with the haka, as well as the highly skilled whētero, or protrusion of the tongue. The woman's role is restricted to moving her hips and using her eyes, either narrowing them or expanding the whites of the eye in pūkana. The use of the tongue was an art form reserved for the men only. While this might appear a limited contribution, it is remarkable what some women can do with their eyes to give full force to the expressions necessary to support a haka.

Apirana Mahuika, a leading chief of Ngāti Porou and an acknowledged expert in te reo me ōna tikanga (the language and its practice), wrote that:

> *A number of haka have been selected . . . to illustrate the similarity in the roles played by men and women in Ngāti Porou on ceremonial occasions — not only as performers, but as composers of these dances. In both the men's and women's haka there is a marked likeness in content, language, rhythm and style of performance and the quality of the Ngāti Porou women's haka is reflected in the fact that today these dances are used by women in other tribal areas.*[1]

Mahuika then goes on to describe the crucial role of women in the composition of some of Ngāti Porou's most famous haka. He notes that:

> *In considering haka compositions, it should be noted that women were often composers of men's haka. The classic haka 'Rūaumoko' . . . is said to have originally been a waiata composed by a woman and it was later modified as a haka by the Rev Mohi Turei. In the case of another Ngāti Porou classic, Te Kiri Ngutu . . . it was composed in reply to a haka composed by a woman.*

Alexander Turnbull Library, PAColl-5584-02

Ngāti Kahungunu in full improvisation as they perform a haka pōwhiri for guests arriving for the wedding of Maude Donnelly in the Hawke's Bay in the early 1900s.

Traditionally, women have been very much a part of the haka. The women most proficient at pūkana were the ones traditionally given the role of manu ngangahu, performing to the side of the main haka troupe. In some instances they were armed, and so protected the flanks of the haka party. They could also act as a prompt to boost the spirit of the performance.

In 1839 John Bidwell, writing in his book *Rambles in New Zealand*, described a haka he observed in Tauranga:

> *I saw this evening a grand war-dance and certainly think it would be sufficient to strike terror into the heart of any man. Imagine a body of about 3,000 nearly naked savages, made as hideous as possible by paint . . . They stood in four close lines, one behind the other, with a solitary leader (as it appeared) in front of the right end of the line. This leader was a woman who excelled in the art of making hideous faces . . .*[2]

Bidwell, transfixed by the spectacle, watched the warriors twist and bend their limbs into different positions. He marvelled at their ability to turn their eyes into the backs of their heads, showing only the whites in the eye sockets. Again the woman leader caught his attention:

> *. . . she was a remarkably handsome woman when her features were in their natural state, but when performing she became more hideous than any person who has not seen savages can possibly imagine: she was really very much like some of the most forbidding of the Hindoo idols — the resemblance to a statue being rendered more perfect by the pupilless eyes, the most disagreeable part of the statue.*[3]

Alexander Turnbull Library, PAColl-0477-03

Woman leading a haka with fierce eye movements (pūkana).

Augustus Earle, Alexander Turnbull Library, PUBL-0022-3

Women in the front ranks of the haka — an engraving taken from an Augustus Earle
drawing, May 1832.

Johannes Andersen described the role of women in the haka at a tribal gathering at
Alexandra (now Pirongia — near Hamilton) in May 1882. The hui had been called by King
Tāwhiao and Wahanui of Waikato and Ngāti Maniapoto, two of the tribes of the Tainui
confederation.

On the last day of the hui the King threw out a challenge to the tribes by throwing a
piece of fern at them. The challenge was immediately seized upon, and men and women
prepared for the haka.

Ngāti Maniapoto lined up in two rows, the men in front and the women at the back. The
male leader began by slapping his knees and chanting as well as rolling his eyes about; this
was followed with a powerful haka:

> *Two native women of rank ran rapidly between and in front of the lines, crying out*
> *as if the fiends possessed them. One very stout chieftainess, as she ran, threw up her*
> *hands, showed the whites of her eyes, and rolled her stomach round and round in the*
> *most startling and alarming manner. The women became even more energetic in their*
> *movements and cries than the men.*[4]

In *Games and Pastimes of the Maori*, Elsdon Best noted that:

> *Both sexes acted as leaders in haka, and women were noted for their lascivious motions*
> *of the onioni [sexual] type. Such leaders usually carried a weapon in the right hand and*
> *indulged in grotesque movements and contortions . . . women preferred the mere, or short*
> *wooden weapon termed meremere.*[5]

The paintings and sketches of early European explorers and sailors also depict women as an integral part of any haka that is captured on canvas or paper. The painting by French artist Louis Auguste de Sainson on board the *Astrolabe* shows a group of Māori doing the haka. Some of the more vigorous haka members are women.

Women's role in haka today

Despite the graphic examples of women traditionally playing leading roles in haka, their role in the haka in contemporary Māori society is more controversial. The noted orator and haka specialist Archdeacon Kīngi Ihaka was concerned that women might be dominating the haka:

> I am positive when we were young women did not perform the haka with the men, that is, in haka taparahi. In my opinion, when [women] perform haka, their actions are too masculine, the conventions, the stamping of the feet, the way the foot is lifted, all these aspects. The women were to the rear. The sole function of the women was to pukana, but they did not say the words of the haka, they did not help the men vocally. That was the exclusive domain of the men. Today, as I watch our performances, the thought occurs to me: I, personally, am not accustomed to the practice of women's voices calling out the lyric along with the men. In some instances the women's voices are louder than those of the men. This is one of my concerns and I disapprove of this aspect of our performance. It is left to the women to give voice to the haka. I was beginning to think that I was mistaken. It is the function of men to give voice to the haka. Perhaps women are permitted vocal support. But not for their voices to predominate, as though it is the women who are leading the haka. That is my greatest concern about haka today.[6]

Courtesy of Te Whānau-a-Apanui Kapa Haka and Te Matatini. Photographer Aaron Smale

New generation of kapa haka exponents, Te Matatini 2005.

Horowaewae (Trevor) Maxwell, leader of Ngāti Rangiwewehi (winners of the national festival in 1983), has views similar to those of Kīngi Ihaka. When asked whether he thought haka was in a healthy state, he replied that it was and added that this included discussion around women taking part in the haka. However, he did qualify his remarks by saying 'I personally would like the men to be judged as doing the haka'.[7]

Ngāpō Wehi, one of the most successful modern kapa haka leaders, has a different view. He observed that when he asked his father's sister, Rawinia Wehi, a renowned haka performer, whether women performed haka in the past, she replied by standing up and '. . . slapping her chest and displaying all the essentials of haka'.

At the national festival in 1980 one group took exception to the rules that forbade women taking part in the haka. The group composed a haka which expressed anger and resentment at the ban. It pointed to the practices and customs of a number of major tribes in which women performed the haka, including the tribes that descended from the *Horouta*, *Te Arawa* and *Mātaatua* waka. As Tīmoti Kāretu noted:

> *It was ironic at this particular festival, in 1980 in Auckland, that two of the women judges performed a haka just to make the point to the national committee that they really were not being endorsed by either the judges or majority of the performing groups. It could be truly said that this policy of the national committee was one of its most unpopular and deserved to be rejected.*[8]

It is interesting to reflect on the clear roles for participation that the Aotearoa New Zealand Army has in its haka for its wahine toa (female soldiers). To acknowledge the prestige and place of women in the army, women begin and end the haka. This contrasts with the ambivalence shown by a number of leading Māori experts and commentators. Moreover,

Courtesy of Ruatahuna Kakahu Mauku. Photographer Aaron Smale

Women from Ruatahuna Kakahu Mauku compete at Te Matatini in 2007.

the current attitudes to women in haka seem to be very much at odds with the observations of nineteenth-century commentators, writers and artists.

There is little doubt that both men and women are essential and complementary ingredients for a successful haka.

Contemporary women composers

Moetū Haangu (Tuini) Ngawai

One of the most gifted contemporary composers of Māori music for haka and kapa haka was Moetū Haangu (Tuini) Ngawai. Tuini was born on 5 May 1910 just north of Tokomaru Bay. When her mother, Te Ipo, was pregnant with her she visited a local tohunga and was told that her child '. . . would be especially gifted in some form of leadership'. Te Ipo had two girls. After 12 months one of the twins died. Moetū was then named Tuini (twin) in recognition that she was one of two. During her lifetime Tuini '. . . was to write 200 songs which are still remembered, most spiritual in their inspiration, but each written for a specific, often pragmatic purpose'[9]

Prior to the Second World War, Tuini moved to Auckland, where she was active in developing her composition techniques. She returned to Tokomaru Bay at the outbreak of the war. Tuini set up the performing group Te Hokowhitu-a-Tū. This group helped Sir Apirana Ngata in his efforts to recruit volunteers for the 28th (Māori) Battalion. As the war progressed they performed for the troops at training, at their departures and at their return from active service.

In October 1943 Tuini was heavily involved with preparing performers for the arrival of the Governor-General and distinguished guests to the Ngarimu Victoria Cross investiture ceremony at Ruatōria. Tuini trained the schools of Ngāti Porou to sing 'Karangatia rā', the song composed by Sir Apirana Ngata for the return of Māori soldiers during the First World War.

Te Hokowhitu-a-Tū performed a number of her well-known tunes, including 'Te Hokowhitu-a-Tū'. She had been composing this song on and off for a couple of years and reportedly in a burst of a couple of minutes finished it off. Sung to the popular American tune immortalised by Glenn Miller's 'In the Mood', it subsequently became a hit with the soldiers as it reminded them of the sacrifices they were about to make. At one part of the tune there is a poignant reminder of Moananui-a-kiwa Ngarimu, who had been posthumously awarded the Victoria Cross, the highest medal of valour of the British Empire for his outstanding bravery in the battle of Point 209, Tebaga Gap, during the Middle East

Tuini Ngawai of Ngāti Porou: a gifted contemporary composer.

Campaign in World War II. She also composed other songs popular with the troops. One such song was a parody of Hitler and Mussolini, 'Hītara Waha Huka'.

Hītara waha huka, upoko mārō	Frothy-mouthed, stubborn-headed Hitler
He tangata tohetohe ki te riri ē	Who keeps fighting on and on!
Hinga atu, hinga mai kore rawa he rerenga	He fell, and fell again in Russia
Ka wiri ana Papa, hei auē auē auē!	They cleaned him up, hei auē auē auē!
	Chorus:
Tū hikitia rā — tū hāpainga rā	Lift right up, lift high up
Te rau o tō patu ki runga i te upoko	My weapon above his head!
Hoatu e tama, karia te kauae	Come on son, and break the jaw
O te purari paka nei a Hītara ē!	Of this cowardly slave, Hitler!
Kua rongo a Mahurinii, kua tata tonu mai	Mussolini has heard, that the Māori Battalion
A te Hokowhitu toa ki Roma ē	Is getting very close to Rome!
Hiki nuku, hiki rangi, kore rawa he rerenga	Move on, move fast, he cannot escape
Ka hiri ōna papa i te mataku ē	His buttocks are shaking with fear!
	Chorus:
Tū hikitia rā — tū hāpainga rā	Lift right up, lift high up
Te rau o tō patu ki runga i te upoko	My weapon above his head!
Hoatu e tama, karia te kauae	Come on son, and break the jaw
O te purari paka nei a Hītara ē	Of this cowardly slave, Hitler!

Ngoi Pewhairangi

Te Kumeroa Ngoingoi Pewhairangi was born in 1921 at Tokomaru Bay on the East Coast and raised in the Ringatū faith. After schooling away from the East Coast she returned and came under the influence of her Aunt, Tuini Ngawai, who was 10 years older than she was.

They both worked in a shearing gang. She and Tuini established a very good relationship which was reflected in her:

> . . . interest in Māori performing arts as a member and leader of Te Hokowhitu-a-Tu Concert Party, which was founded by Tuini Ngawai in 1939. During the early 1940s they travelled around New Zealand entertaining and raising funds for the war effort. Ngoi was groomed by Tuini Ngawai in performance, composition and leadership, and she tutored and led the group on many occasions.[10]

Ngoi was a spontaneous composer and seemed to do her best when working with a kindred spirit. One such kindred spirit was Dalvanius Prime from Taranaki who came to visit in the early 1980s and struck up a great friendship with Ngoi. One of the outstanding products of this relationship was the composition of the song 'Poi e', which was recorded by Dalvanius and the Patea Māori Club and went on to sell 15,000 copies.

8

War and haka

War and the price of citizenship

The two world wars were a time for Māori to demonstrate their contribution towards the defence of the nation and to mark their coming of age as fully contributing citizens. That Aotearoa New Zealand society and its decision-makers in Parliament were slow in recognising the sacrifices made by Māori soldiers seemed not to deter Māori from wanting to serve the nation.

As well as its role in rousing passion before battle, the haka has been used by Māori soldiers at various times as a means of building spirit, teamwork and cohesion in the armed forces. As Barry Mitcalfe observed:

> . . . *each of the European wars has seen haka adapted for the occasion with appropriate references to Kruger [the Boer leader], to the Kaiser [Kaiser Wilhelm was the German emperor during the First World War] and to Hitler.*[1]

As Mitcalfe also noted, it is quite easy to adapt a haka by just changing a word or two.

Māori participation in nineteenth-century conflicts

Māori soldiers have served the Crown since 1845–46, during the wars in northern Aotearoa New Zealand. Hone Heke, one of the leading chiefs in the region, and a signatory to the Treaty of Waitangi on 6 February 1840, had quickly become disenchanted with the actions of the British in upholding the Treaty. To bring attention to his dissatisfaction with their shortcomings he chopped down the British flagpole on Kororāreka hill (in present-day Russell). The flagpole was re-erected and he chopped it down again. He chopped it down a third time and soon after, with the support of another doughty northern chief, Kāwiti, attacked and burnt the settlement of Kororāreka.

The British were supported in their efforts to bring Heke and Kāwiti under control by another of the region's leading chiefs, Tāmati Waka Nene. After a number of skirmishes, the protagonists met at a battle site called Ōhaeawai. Here the old fighting chief Kāwiti and 100 men set their defences and subsequently repulsed a superior British force.

Horatio Gordon Robley, Alexander Turnbull Library, A-080-051

Serried ranks of warriors with arms, performing a haka peruperu in front of Maketu Pa, 1865.

Killed in the attack and the skirmishes preceding it were a number of Ngāpuhi from the Hokianga, who were said to be supporting the British but who, it is claimed, could equally have been there to settle old scores. Immediately after the attack Kāwiti is said to have composed this haka peruperu:

E tama te uaua	Men of sinew
E tama te mārōrō	Men of strength
Ina hoki rā te tohu	Behold the source
O te uaua	And symbol of power
Kei taku ringa, e mau ana	Here in my hand
Te upoko	I hold the head
O te Kawau Tahika	Of Te Kawau Tahika

During the turbulent early years of Māori–European interaction the haka was used to boost adrenalin and build up passion and commitment before battle. It was also commonly used to intimidate and pour vitriol on the enemy.

The First World War

The opportunity for Māori troops to give formal expression to the haka was taken on Gallipoli during August 1915. On the night of 6 August, Māori soldiers of the 1st Māori Contingent went into battle on the bleak and blood-soaked ridges of Gallipoli. The peninsula, which was to bind together in blood and sacrifice the two young nations of Australia and Aotearoa New Zealand, heard for the first time on foreign soil the battle cries of the sons and warriors of Tūmatauenga (the god of war).

Members of the Pioneer Battalion performing a haka for visiting New Zealand ministers Massey and Ward at Bois-de-Warnimont, France, 1916.

This proud and historic moment was captured by Major Te Rangi Hiroa (later Sir Peter Buck), Medical Officer to the 1st Māori Contingent, as the soldiers carried out a night attack on Sari Bair ridge. He wrote in his diary that he knew that a Turkish trench had been captured in the darkness at the point of the bayonet. He continued:

> *But more wonderful to me was that the night air was broken vigorously by the Māori war cry of 'Ka mate, ka mate! Ka ora, ka ora!* [2]

Hardly had the excitement died down than the sequence was repeated on another part of the battlefield. Even at this distance in time from the event, one can sense the pride in his words as he noted:

> *. . . my heart thrilled at the sound of my mother tongue resounding up the slopes of Sari Bair.* [3]

Ironically, few realise the enormous difficulties faced by Māori politicians in Aotearoa New Zealand as they tried to persuade the British authorities to accept a volunteer Māori unit for the war. Up until this time, resistance by the British was based on the nineteenth-century idea that black or coloured soldiers could not be pitted against European foes. Even when permission was granted by the Imperial General Staff in London for a unit to be raised, it was not to be what Māori desperately sought — a full combat unit. Rather, the 1st Māori Contingent was raised and trained as pioneer troops to dig trenches and carry out the myriad of menial tasks needed to support an army at war.

Later on during the First World War a Māori Pioneer Battalion was raised and served with distinction on the Western Front in France. On numerous occasions, when Aotearoa New Zealand and other dignitaries visited the Aotearoa New Zealand troops, invariably the Māori soldiers would be called upon to perform the haka. Few visitors could resist being impressed with the energy and vitality brought by these soldiers of the Empire, fighting and dying 14,000 kilometres from their homeland.

The Second World War

Shortly after the outbreak of the Second World War, at the end of 1939, the 28th (Māori) Battalion was formed and its members gathered in Palmerston North to train for overseas deployment. Soon after its inception the battalion formed a concert party. In addition, because each of the battalion's companies was made up

28th (Māori) Battalion soldiers perform haka in Cairo during the Second World War.

Alexander Turnbull Library, F-1229-DA

Haka in the desert performed by 28th (Māori) Battalion soldiers during the Second World War.

of men from distinct tribal areas and tribal groupings, each company was able to showcase its own tribal haka. Often the competitions among the companies were fierce, as each tribe strived to assert pre-eminence.

The opportunities for a spontaneous haka during battle would have been limited. Perhaps the knowledge that a bullet could strike from any direction reduced the desire to cluster together to offer a challenge to an enemy position or to advancing enemy troops! However, on numerous occasions before planned attacks the soldiers would either carry out karakia (prayer) individually or in small groups or they would quietly sing the hymn: 'Auē e Ihu' ('Death where is thy sting').

One example of a haka being performed during battle occurred in early November 1942, during Operation Supercharge as the British Eighth Army was trying to break out from El Alamein in the latter stages of the Desert Campaign. The 28th (Māori) Battalion was assigned to support 151st Brigade of the 51st British Division. The battle was intense and battalions had to fight all the way to the objectives under strong German resistance. Lieutenant-Colonel Charles Bennett in command of the Māori Battalion described a particularly intense engagement by B Company. At one spot the company was opposed by a wall of fire. Bennett describes how they all broke into the haka 'Ka Mate!' and then charged the enemy positions with fixed bayonets. It was, he said: '. . . the most spirited attack he had taken part in'.[4]

During the campaigns in Greece, Crete, North Africa and Italy, the concert party played a major role during periods when the battalion was out of battle. This was especially the case when the battalion was playing rugby. In the Middle East where large concentrations

of British, South African, Australian and New Zealand troops were concentrated there was inevitably an opportunity between battles to play rugby. When a team from the Māori Battalion was playing, the cheering soldiers would often break into a haka to urge on their compatriots.

Post-World War II deployments

The idea of having a Māori concert party took hold in the armed forces after the Second World War and became a fixture during the period of Aotearoa New Zealand's deployment into South-east Asia (as described on page 16). Consequently, the haka and the Māori concert party became very much entrenched in the minds of the commanders as a vehicle to win the hearts and minds of the local people, as well as a means of lifting the morale of all the Aotearoa New Zealand troops.

With the deployment of small contingents to South Vietnam and the incorporation of Aotearoa New Zealand rifle companies into Australian battalions, the opportunities for formal concert parties were limited, although from time to time Aotearoa New Zealand soldiers could stump up with a haka. Occasionally, too, Aotearoa New Zealanders brought in to entertain the troops would have a Māori troupe, who would liven up the crowd with haka.

Following the withdrawal of Aotearoa New Zealand troops from South Vietnam in the early 1970s, few soldiers could see any opportunities ahead for the deployment of Aotearoa New Zealand forces. However, it is fair to say that in the past 15 years Aotearoa New Zealand's peace-keeping role has grown dramatically, calling for a different kind of training and the need to develop an esprit de corps for these difficult operational assignments.

Courtesy of the NZDF

Soldiers from the 3rd NZ Battalion group (NZBatt3) perform their battalion haka to welcome a dignitary to their operations in Suai, East Timor.

The army redefined

The army's efforts to reorientate its soldiers and train them for their, at times, hugely frustrating peace-keeping roles required the development of different skills to cope with an operational environment far removed from the one which the jungle-trained soldiers of the 1960s and 1970s faced. Critical to this rebuilding was the idea of strengthening the ethos and cultural robustness of soldiers who would now have to deal with ethnically diverse populations in the Middle East, the Balkans and countries like East Timor.

In the early 1990s the Chief of General Staff of the army, Major-General Anthony Birks, decided to formally incorporate a greater degree of tikanga (protocol) in army life. In 1995 the army adopted the identity of Ngāti Tūmatauenga, the Tribe of the War God. This was an extraordinary event in our history, greeted with little fuss by the public at large. It also was a realistic response to the relationships forged between Māori and non-Māori in the service of the nation.

In May 1997 Chief of General Staff Major-General Piers Reid commissioned kaumātua Te Keepa Takataka-o-rangi Stirling and his brother Rōpata Wahawaha Stirling of Ngāti Porou and Te Whānau-a-Apanui to write a haka for the army.

In the past the army had unwittingly used a haka that incorporated elements of another haka, 'Rūaumoko'. This haka is sacred to the people of the East Coast and the eastern Bay of Plenty, and Māoridom in general would consider it a bad omen should it be performed incorrectly. Rūaumoko is the god of earthquakes and volcanoes, and it was considered inappropriate to include elements about him in a haka dedicated to Tūmatauenga, the god of war. The Stirling brothers were asked to devise a haka that would embody the history and spirit of the Aotearoa New Zealand Army and its unique warrior spirit. In composing the haka the brothers were guided by the ethos and spirit or wairua of the army. Te Keepa attributed much to the experience of his brother Rōpata, who as a very young man had served with the 28th (Māori) Battalion and fought in the battle of Monte Cassino. Te Keepa said that the haka spoke about:

> . . . *the extreme terrain, the deep frustrations, the hurt, the suffering and all the uncertainty for a soldier in time of battle.*[5]

While the haka was completed in October 1997 and performed for the first time then, it was not publicly launched until 30 January 1998 on the army's national marae at Waiouru. The army describes its haka as:

Soldiers perform the NZ Army haka in front of the NZ Army Marae in Waiouru.

. . . a haka taparahi (performed without weapons) and is a tribute to those soldiers who have passed on. It is intended to be performed by all ranks regardless of race or gender, in uniform and not in traditional Māori dress. The reason for this is that as a [Aotearoa] New Zealand Army we did not and do not fight in, or with, traditional Māori dress and weapons. Our soldiers fought and died in the uniform of our Army. To acknowledge the mana wahine (prestige of women) in the Army, female soldiers begin and end the haka.[6]

In handing over the completed haka to the army, Te Keepa Stirling admonished them to consider carefully when it might be used. One of the first non-army occasions on which it was performed was at the funeral of Sir Charles Bennett, who had been the last surviving commander of the 28th (Māori) Battalion. The haka is entitled 'Tū Taua a Tūmatauenga' ('The fighting columns of Tūmatauenga'), and it is now a standard part of the formal ceremonies to farewell and greet soldiers leaving for and returning from overseas deployments.

At its public launch, Camp Commander Colonel Ian Marshall explained that the haka could be performed anywhere in the world, by any soldier in the Aotearoa New Zealand army, without any special equipment and that it reflected the multicultural ethos of the army. (The last point is an interesting observation, as one would have thought that in fact the haka represented the bicultural nature of the Treaty of Waitangi partnership between Māori and non-Māori!)

Major-General Piers Reid, the Chief of General Staff, in his last year of service would have been proud to have taken the army another step along the road to harmonising the potential of his troops while at the same time respecting their differences.

General Reid's successor, Chief of General Staff Major-General Maurice Dodson, saw the naming of the army after the god of war as a way of recognising the place of the Māori warrior in the Aotearoa New Zealand Army. He described an incident when visiting the Aotearoa New Zealand Special Air Service in Kuwait in 1998. Some 4000 troops were near the airfield where he was going to land. When he arrived the SAS troopers were lined up beside the airfield, and when he reached the tarmac they exploded into the haka 'Ka Mate!'. The impact of this was immediate as troops on the airfield stopped, awestruck, by the spectacle.

When General Dodson took command of the army in 1998 he decided to take the concept of Ngāti Tūmatauenga a step further. Under his guidance the army fashioned an extraordinary vision statement:

When the [Aotearoa] New Zealand Army was formed it was based on British military tradition. We want to meld that with Maori tradition, and so form something that is uniquely Aotearoa New Zealand . . . We want an organisation based primarily on tikanga . . . Over time Ngati Tumatauenga and the [Aotearoa] New Zealand Army will be synonymous.[7]

All Aotearoa New Zealand soldiers are expected to learn this haka, and it, along with the wero or challenge, has now become an integral part of the rituals of the army, such as formal farewell or welcoming parades. It is a joy to watch Māori and Pākehā Aotearoa New Zealanders standing side by side executing a perfectly performed haka!

Tū tauā a Tūmatauenga
(The fighting columns of Tūmatauenga — the war god)

Wāhine toa	**Female soldiers**
E koro mā, e kui mā, e tama mā	Old men, old women
Haere rā, haere rā, haere rā	Thrice farewell
Kaea	**Leader**
Taringa whakarongo, kia rite, kia rite, kia mau	Listen, be alert, be prepared, stand steady
Torona kei waho	Extend the arms
Ararā ki ngā ope tū tauā	Be warned of the fighting columns
a Tūmatauenga ē	of Tūmatauenga
I āhaha!	I awaken

(The group lower their heads to the sound of the pūrerehua — the moth wing sound heard at birth and at death — signifying the 'Last Post' being sounded.)

Rōpū	**Group**
Ko mātou ā koutou mōrehurehu	We are your descendants of today
e whai ake nei	
I tae koutou ki te mura o te ahi	You arrived at the flames of hell
He kōhatuhatu, reporepo, kirikiri, paruparu,	Rocks, swamp, sand, mud, jungle
ngahere, tomo tauā e, I āhaha!	and built-up areas, I awaken
Kaea	**Leader**
I tukua ā koutou tinana hei tūkinotanga mā	You gave up your bodies to be abused by
te hoariri	the enemy
E, hei ora nei mātou e whai ake nei	that we might live on
Rōpū	**Group**
Tatangi nei ngā matā me te whewhio	The bullets and ricochets sing
Paku korara, ka mate, ka mate, auē taukiri ē	Bombs explode, 'tis death, 'tis death,
	alas the grief
Paku tāporepore auē, ka mau te wehi!	Artillery rounds cartwheeling, oh, the fear
He pokokohua whenua paku ake e, i āhaha!	The cursed earth explodes, I awaken
He kiri mamae, au, au, au	The skin is in pain
I kō taku toto rangatira ka maringi noa	My chiefly blood runs out
He papa, tuakana, teina, whanaunga noa	Fathers, older brothers, younger
	brothers and relatives
Kua ngaro ki te pō, auē, auē, taukiri e!	Lost to the night, alas the grief
Kaea	**Leader**
Mate atu, he toa, ara mai rā he toa	One warrior dies, another rises
Moana Ngārimu ngā ū te wikitōria nui	Moana Ngārimu is awarded the Victoria Cross

Rōpū	Group
He rā, he wiki, he marama, he tau	A day, a week, a month, a year
Mai i te awatea ki te pō, i te pō, ki te haeata	from daybreak to nightfall, from night to dawn
Ko te rōpū o Tūmatauenga	The fighting columns of Tūmatauenga
kei te mura rawa o te ahi	were at the fires of hell
Ka whawhai tonu mō ake tonu atu ē	They fought on and on
I te hekenga atu o te rā	At the going down of the sun
E kore rawa koutou e kaumātuatia	You will not achieve the mantle of
	aged and respected mentors
Kahore hoki koutou e warewaretia	But you shall not be forgotten
E te rōpū tū tauā o	For we are the fighting columns of
Tūmatauenga, o Aotearoa	Tūmatauenga of Aotearoa New Zealand
Auē, auē, kei wareware tātou	Alas, alas, lest we forget

Wāhine toa	Female soldiers
E koro mā, e kui mā, e tama mā	Old men, old women, young men
Haere, haere, haere atu koutou	Thrice farewell
Haere atu koutou i te huanui i te papatauira	Farewell as you tread the pathway
E te tapuwae kauika tangata	The footsteps that all men must take
Takoto mai koutou i te urunga e kore e nekehia	Rest yourselves on the pillow
	that cannot be moved
I te moenga e kore e hikitia	On the pillow that cannot be carried away
Haere, haere, haere	Thrice farewell
Ka maumahara tonu tātou ki a koutou e!	We shall remember you

(This is the karanga whakamutunga, the final farewell tribute given by four female soldiers. The final line is taken from Binyon's lines 'We shall remember them'.)

The 8th NZDF Provincial Reconstruction Team contingent performs a haka to the departing contingent as they assume command of the mission in Afghanistan.

Ngarimu Victoria Cross

Commemoration and celebrations

In March 1943, in the North African desert at Point 209, Tebaga Gap, Tunisia, thousands of miles from home, Second-Lieutenant Moananui-a-kiwa Ngarimu gave his life in a desperate struggle to beat off a last-ditch counter-attack by a German force. Earlier in the afternoon he had led his platoon against German soldiers entrenched in their positions.

Throughout the night the situation changed as each side fought for control of the hill. As the dawn emerged Ngarimu and his remaining soldiers were clinging to their positions. By now they had run out of grenades and Ngarimu had told his men to throw stones. The Germans tried one more attack and in rushing to the defence of his men and the positions they held Ngarimu was killed. For his outstanding bravery on that day he was awarded the Victoria Cross, the highest medal of honour of the British Empire.

Moana was born at Whareponga on the East Coast on 7 April 1919. On the beach not far from his birthplace warriors used to be trained in the arts of war. His father Hāmuera Meketu Ngarimu was of Ngāti Porou and his mother Maraea was from Te Whānau-a-Apanui. The commemorations of Moana's death and the celebrations for his life and the award of the Victoria Cross went on for months, culminating in the gathering of the tribes at Ruatōria on 6 October 1943 to witness the handing over of his posthumously awarded medal for valour to his parents.

The preparations by Ngāti Porou for the big day went on for weeks. Marae readied themselves for the influx of thousands of visitors. Rehearsals and practices took place under the watchful eyes of Sir Apirana himself and Ngoi Pewhairangi and others.

The occasion of the posthumous award of the Victoria Cross to the parents of Moana Ngarimu gave Ngāti Porou the opportunity to showcase its prowess in performing both men's and women's haka taparahi. Sir Āpirana Ngata presented most of the outstanding examples of these haka.

In a report describing the hui ILG Sutherland noted that:

The actual investiture ceremony was preceded by a four hour programme of entertainment. . . . Sir Apirana Ngata was at the microphone . . . explaining the items presented. . . . The reception was notable for the revival and presentation of a number of famous haka Peruperu and songs as well as for a number of new compositions, and the Māori gift for the topical adaptation and composition was evident.[8]

Second Lieutenant Moananui-a-kiwa Ngarimu (20 years old), awarded a posthumous Victoria Cross for bravery, Tebaga Gap, Tunisia, March 1943.

Alexander Turnbull Library, PAColl-6301-60

Ngāti Porou women performing at a hui in Ruatoria, October 1943, held to award the Victoria Cross posthumously to the parents of Second Lieutenant Moananui-a-kiwa Ngarimu. Sir Apirana Ngata is in the foreground.

Women's haka taparahi pōwhiri (welcome)

The haka taparahi below was especially written for the occasion and performed by the women. It was addressed to the guest of honour, the Governor-General. In the pōwhiri the women pose the rhetorical question: Who is it that travels towards them? They reply that it is the Governor coming to Uepōhatu marae, for the occasion of the sacred hui, to bestow the Victoria Cross on the parents of the young warrior who died on the battlefields so far from home.

The pōwhiri tells of Moana's death and asks for a sharp stone that the women may lacerate themselves as a mark of their sorrow for Moana and to disfigure their bodies that once he looked upon in his lifetime. The imagery here is one of sorrow and distress at the loss of a fine man — someone's relation, someone's loved one. The traditional practice of laceration on the death of a loved one served the purpose of expressing grief and at the same time distancing future suitors.

The pōwhiri ends with a call to the Governor-General, an almost hopeless plea for him to staunch the unceasing flow of tears caused by Moana's death.

Nō wai te motokā
e topa mai ngā rori?
Auē! Nōu nei Kāwana
Tika mai nei taua, i nawa!
Auē! Auē! Auē! Hā!
Auē! Auē! Auē! Hā!

Whose is the motorcar speeding
hither along the highway?
Is it thine, O Governor,
coming direct to me.

Maehe te marama	March was the month
i haere ai a Moana	when Moana scaled the hill
Auē! I piki ai rā i te hiwi	Alas! It was to his
Ki te mate i taua, i nawa	death he ascended.
Auē! Auē! Auē! Hā!	
Auē! Auē! Auē! Hā!	
Homai he mata,	Hand me the sharp obsidian
kia haehae au	to lacerate myself
Auē! Kia kotia i te kiri	That I may disfigure the form
I awhi ai taua, i nawa	you have often embraced.
Auē! Auē! Auē! Hā!	
Auē! Auē! Auē! Hā!	
Māu rā e Kāwana	It may be that you can, O Governor,
E hohoki ai te roimata!	stem this flow of tears,
Aue! I maringi nei me he wai	Which flows as a torrent
Ki te ipo i taua, i nawa	for my loved one, alas!
Auē! Auē! Auē! Hā!	
Auē! Auē! Auē! Hā!	

'Te Urunga Tū, Te Urunga Pae'

This haka pōwhiri links the famous chiefly brothers Porourangi and Tahu through a woman called Hamoterangi. She and Porourangi were married. When he died she married the other brother Tahu and moved with him to the South Island. Porourangi and Hamoterangi's descendants became Ngāti Porou and Tahu and Hamoterangi's descendants became Ngāi Tahu: Ngāti Porou being the second-largest tribe in the country and Ngāi Tahu being the wealthiest.

It is a lighter-hearted haka of welcome in which a fantail imbued with its twittery, cheerfulness celebrates the lives of these ancestors and bids welcome to friends from near and far.

Tena e whiua	Begin with a swing
Taku pohiri i rere atu ra	My call has gone forth
Ki te hiku o te ika	To the tail of the fish
Te puku o te whenua	To the belly of the land
Te Pane o te motu	To the head of the island
Ki te whakawhititanga i Raukawa	Thence by crossing at Raukawa
KI te Waipounamu e	Top the land of the greenstone
E i aha tera!	The call has gone forth!
E haramai koe i te pohiritanga	So come ye at the welcome
A taku manu	Given by my bird
E haramai koe i te pohiritanga	Respond ye to the cry
A taku manu	Of my bird's welcome!
He tiwaka ahau na Maui	I am the fantail of Maui
Tiori rau e he ha!	Chirping relentlessly to and from

He tiwaiwaka ahau na Maui	I am the fantail of Maui
Tiori rau e he ha!	Gaily singing, darting here and there!
Te urunga tu, te urunga pae	It enters vertically, it enters horizontally
Te urunga matiketike	It enters erect!
Te urunga tu, te urunga pae	It enters vertically, it enters horizontally
Te urunga matiketike	It enters erect!
Ko tohou aro i tahuri mai	You will turn yourself to me
Ko toku aro i tahuri atu	And I will turn myself to you
Takina ko koe! Takina ko au!	There is your challenge to me
Ko tohou aro i tahuri mai	You will turn yourself to me
Ko toku aro i tahuri atu	And I will turn myself to you
Takina ko koe! Takina ko au!	There is your challenge to me
Porou koa!	Tis Porou indeed!
Ko Hamo te wahine koa!	And Hamo his consort too!
Ko Tahu koa!	Tis Tahu indeed!
Ko Hamo te wahine koa!	And Hamo his consort also!
Nana i tohatoha ki Niu Tireni	They have broadcast their progeny all over
Ka hipoki!	New Zealand!
Haere mai! Haere mai!	Welcome to you, welcome to you
Haere mai! Haere mai!	Welcome to you, welcome to you
Ki taku hui! Hei!	Come to our hui.

'Ka Panapana'

This is a classic women's haka of welcome and was one of the key items performed by the women of Ngāti Porou at the Victoria Cross investiture ceremony. Sir Āpirana modified the haka to refer disparagingly to Hitler. The ranks of performers faced the dignitaries on a temporary stage and went through their paces.

Arara! Ka panapana, Āhaha!	Lo, it is throbbing! Āhaha!
Ka rekareka tonu taku ngākau	My heart is throbbing delighted
Ki ngā mana ririki i pōhatu whakapiri	With the common people like stones stuck together
Kia haramai te takitini,	Who have come in their multitudes
Kia haramai te takimano,	Who have come in their thousands
Kia paretaitokotia ki Rāwhiti!	And alighted upon the Eastern sea.
Hī! Hā!	Hī! Hā!
He mamae, he mamae! Āhaha!	Alas, there is a multitude of pain!
Ka haere, ka haere taku pōwhiri	My call of welcome goes out
Ki te Tai Whakarunga!	To the Southern Sea!

Hoki mai, hoki mai taku tinana!	But alas comes back to me!
Ka haere, ka haere taku pōwhiri	My words of welcome go out
Ki te Tai Whakararo!	To the Northern Sea!
Hoki mai, hoki mai taku tinana!	But again come back to me!
Kia huri au ki Te Tai Whakatū a Kupe	So I turn to the sea which Kupe raised up
Ki te Tai o Matawhero i motu mai!	To the sea which breaks at Matawhero!
E ko Hītara ki roto ki aku ringa,	There is Hitler within my embrace,
Kutia rawatia kia pari tona ihu!	Where I will crush him and break him!
Hī! Hā! Auahi ana! Kss! Kss hei!	Hī! Hā! It is fitting!
Kia whakangā hoki au i ahau	Now let me pause and rest awhile
I auē! Hei!	Down, down to the ground.[9]

'Rūaumoko'

The pièce de résistance for the investiture programme was the haka 'Rūaumoko'. According to information given to Āpirana Mahuika by his father, Hāmana Mahuika, a renowned Ngāti Porou cultural expert, this classic Ngāti Porou haka was said to have been composed by a woman in the eighteenth century and '. . . like other old compositions, it contains classical allusions which are obscure to all but students of classical Māori'.[10] It was later modified by the Anglican clergyman, Mohi Turei.

Ko Rūaumoko e ngunguru nei!	Hark to the rumbling of
	the Earthquake Demon!
Hī Au! Au! Auē hā!	Hī Au! Au! Auē hā!
Ko Rūaumoko e ngunguru nei!	It is Rūaumoko who trembles and stirs!
Hī Au! Au! Auē hā!	Hī Au! Au! Auē hā!
I āhaha!	I āhaha!
E ko te rākau a	It is the rod of Tū the Suspended One!
Tūngāwerewere I āhaha!	
He rākau tapu nā Tūtaua ki a Uenuku.	A sacred rod given by Tūtaua to Uenuku.
I patukia ki te tipua o Rangitōpeka,	It strikes the monster Rangitōpeka,
Pakaru te upoko o Rangitōpeka,	It breaks Rangitōpeka's head
Patua ki waenganui	Splitting the ridge of Hikurangi,
o te tau ki Hikurangi,	from where a carved rock emerges.
He toka whakairo e tū ake nei.	
He atua! He tangata! He atua!	It is divine! Human! Divine!
He tangata, ho!	Human, oh!
He atua, he atua Tauparetaitoko,	Divine! divine! strange Paretaitoko
Kia kitea e Paretaitoko te whare haunga!	Paretaitoko sees the musky house
I āhaha!	I āhaha!
Kia whakatete mai o rei, he kurī! Au!	Where the dog is ready to bite! Ah!
I āhaha!	I āhaha!
Nā wai parehua taku hope	In my ecstasy I see the sky enflamed
kia whakakā te rangi	
Kia tare au! Hī!	I gasp for breath! Ah!
etc. . . .	etc. . . .

Kapa haka and Te Matatini

Every two years in halls, clubs and marae throughout New Zealand and Australia, Māori gather to begin the two-year journey to win the right to represent their region at the biennial national kapa haka festival, Te Matatini. Kapa means 'to stand in a row' and haka means 'to dance'.[1]

Held in various forms since 1972, this has become the premier showcase for kapa haka (haka groups). The event provides an opportunity for a select handful of groups to perform before their peers and thousands of mainly Māori spectators. The opportunity to demonstrate prowess at haka in its various forms has become an essential part in the life of Māori communities.

The history of the national kapa haka festival

The festival had its beginnings in a resolution passed by the Māori Purposes Fund Board on 11 August 1964 to consider sponsoring prizes in a national cultural competition.[2] Some five years later, in 1969, the idea gained support at a national development conference and in the following year the sub-committee on Polynesian entertainment of the Tourism Development Council endorsed the idea of holding regional Māori festivals and an annual Polynesian Festival. It was also recommended that a committee be established to begin the festivals on a regional and national basis.

The establishment of the Polynesian Festival Committee was confirmed and it was agreed that the inaugural Polynesian Festival would be held in 1972. The first two annual New Zealand Polynesian festivals were held in Rotorua in 1972 and 1973. In both these years Pacific Island groups took part. After 1973 the Pacific Island element was not continued.

The inaugural winning group was Waihirere; coached at that time by Bub and Nan Wehi who for the last 35 years have been closely involved with the festival competitions; initially, as performers and more latterly as tutors.

Their track record at the Aotearoa Māori Performing Arts Festival is a testament to their impeccable standards. Bub and Nan are the only tutors in the country to have ever won at the Festival five times, three times with the Auckland-based club, Te Waka Huia (1986, 92, 96) and twice with Gisborne-based group, Waihirere Māori Group (1972, 79).[3]

After Bub and Nan Wehi left Waihirere to live in Auckland where they began the equally successful Te Waka Huia Group, the Waihirere Group under the leadership of George and Tangiwai Ria went on to win a further three times in 1988, 1998 and 2002.

Ngāti Poneke kapa haka group at the National Polynesian Festival, Heretaunga (Hastings), 1983.

After 1973, the Polynesian Festival Committee decided to make the competitions biennial. In the early years the competing teams numbered between 13 and 15. Also in the early years the competitions were funded by the groups themselves with the host areas bearing the majority of the brunt of the growing costs of hosting the festival supplemented by funds from a variety of sources including the Department of Māori Affairs and its successor agency Te Puni Kōkiri.

In 1996 the Polynesian Festival Committee changed its name to the Aotearoa Traditional Māori Performing Arts Society and was registered as an incorporated society. Two years later it was funded by the Ministry for Culture and Heritage and that funding continues today.

In December 2003 Māori linguist and academic Professor Wharehuia Milroy renamed the performing arts festival Te Matatini. The words mean the 'many faces' and reflect the objective of performing arts. As Professor Milroy explains:

> *Māori performing arts bring together people of all ages, all backgrounds, all beliefs, Māori and non Māori alike; participants and observers. When I look at those performing I see many faces, young and old — Te Matatini.*[4]

Broadening objectives of Te Matatini

The original objective was simply to hold a festival of kapa haka on a biennial basis. However, over the past few years the objectives have broadened to encompass not only an economically successful biennial festival, but also to develop regional plans for fostering and growing interest in kapa haka, to advocate on behalf of groups to open up opportunities locally and internationally, and to hold exhibitions as part of the national festival.

The Te Matatini National Committee, the governance board of Te Matatini comprising 14 regional representatives, has out of necessity over recent years been forced to become economically more self-sufficient. At the festival held at Ōrākei, Auckland, in 2002, it was reported that the event had run at a loss of $1 million. Trevor Maxwell, leader of the champion Ngāti Rangiwewehi kapa haka of Rotorua and a vocal critic of the way in which the festival had been run, suggested that as a consequence of the losses the next festival may have to be delayed.

One of the casualties of the fall-out was Tīmoti Kāretu, who resigned as chairman of the festival committee. Over the next 12 months the committee struggled to work its way through the difficulties imposed by the losses. Another casualty of the efforts of the festival committee was the withdrawal of the Te Arawa teams from festival planning.

It is understood that the major sticking point was the proposal by new management and the new chairman, Tama Huata, to ask kapa haka teams to sign over ownership of songs written for the competitions. As a consequence Ngāti Rangiwewehi and Te Mātārae-i-o-Rehu boycotted the 2005 national festival and Te Arawa held its own competitions.

The absence of these two top sides from the biennial festival was keenly felt by the other top teams. The winning team at the 2005 Te Matatini Festival was Te Whānau-a-Apanui. In one of their items they called for Te Arawa to rejoin the competition.

In 2006 two teams were chosen from Te Arawa but again Ngāti Rangiwewehi and Te Mātārae-i-o-Rehu opted out of the national festival. All parties hope for an amicable resolution of these difficulties in the near future.

HAKA: *A Living Tradition*

Notwithstanding these hiccups the festival has been highly successful, providing a platform for showcasing Māori culture and a crucial vehicle for ensuring the survival of the culture. It has also made a major contribution to the general economies where it has been held. At the 1998 festival in Wellington an estimated 52,000 people crammed the Trentham racecourse grounds to attend the three-day event, with teams coming from all over New Zealand and from Australia. The cost of running the event was approximately $1 million and it was estimated that a further $15 million was injected into the local economy.

Successful kapa haka teams

Since its inception in 1972 Te Matatini has been dominated by a small handful of teams led by experienced leaders. Successful teams at previous festivals are set out below:

Location	Year	Group
Rotorua	1972	Waihīrere
Rotorua	1973	Māwai Hākona
Whangārei	1975	Te Roopu Manutaki
Te Tairāwhiti	1977	Te Kotahitanga o Waitaha
Wellington	1979	Waihīrere
Auckland	1981	Taniwharau
Hastings	1983	Ngāti Rangiwewehi
Christchurch	1986	Te Waka Huia
Whangārei	1988	Waihīrere
Waitangi	1990	Te Roopu Manutaki
Ngāruawāhia	1992	Te Waka Huia
Hāwera	1994	Te Waka Huia
Rotorua	1996	Ngāti Rangiwewehi
Wellington	1998	Waihīrere
Ngāruawāhia	2000	Te Mātārae-i-o-Rehu
Ōrākei	2002	Waihīrere
Palmerston North	2005	Te Whānau-a-Apanui
Palmerston North	2007	Whāngārā-mai-tawhiti

Te Matatini performance programme

The competition programme for Te Matatini follows a set format. Timings must be adhered to and any overruns will result in penalties that could mean the difference between winning and losing. In the two years of preparation teams know exactly what they have to do. And yet remarkably no matter how much they train, teams can go over the mark and lose points. The programme and items to be performed are as follows:

Performance items

These are the six disciplines, described opposite, that each kapa haka group must execute in their performance bracket. They are commonly known as the aggregate items. There are prizes for each category. In addition, there are prizes for the best male and female leaders, and for dress.

1. **Whakaeke — Entry** (Trophy: Te Whānau o Waipāreira)

   The whakaeke or entrance introduces the group and is often an attention grabber. It usually links the group to the region and its host. The whakaeke is a highly choreographed item these days, it's designed to grab the attention of the audience and the judges and lets the people know just who they are.

2. **Waiata tawhito** (Trophy: Te Kani Te Ua)

   Waiata tawhito can come in many forms including pōkeka, ngeri, mōteatea, pātere, pao. Waiata tawhito are chants performed in a traditional Māori tone. You'll see lots of spontaneous and individual expression from the performers with evocative and poetic lyrics. The mōteatea can be stirring.

3. **Poi** (Trophy: Te Kaunihera a Rohe Māori o Aotea)

   This item demonstrates the dexterity required when using poi. The rhythm of the poi helps to keep the tempo and beat of the song while demonstrating the meaning of the lyrics. Always popular as the women are able to show their skills. This discipline can take a number of forms from the single short poi to the difficult double long.

Entertainment is in the blood: Howard Morrison Junior, Polynesian Festival, Christchurch, 1986.

4. **Waiata-ā-ringa — Action song** (Trophy: Ikaroa)

   Waiata-ā-ringa are songs that use traditional hand and body movements to convey the meaning of words. It provides a lovely contrast to the mōteatea. These items usually have contemporary tunes, beautiful rich harmonies and graceful movement.

5. **Haka** (Trophy: Te Ngākau Aroha o Te Waipounamu)

   Haka is an aggressive posture dance and is always eagerly awaited. Like the poi, it too can take a number of forms. Haka taparahi and haka peruperu are just two variations. A common thread emerging at the festival is that the haka tackles the contentious issues of the day head on.

6. **Whakawātea — Exit** (Trophy: Wi Te Tau Huata)

   The Whakawātea ends the group's performance with it exiting the stage from the right, left or centre. Once again important as the kapa haka strive to finish as strongly as they began and attempt to leave a lasting impression.[5]

Judging for excellence

In any competition the judges have a critical role to play in ensuring that the performances are judged according to an understood set of criteria. Because of the highly competitive

nature of kapa haka competitions judges come under enormous scrutiny from coaches, performers and members of a highly vocal public. For these reasons it is important that there is an agreed process, rules and competent judges to bring credibility to the competitions.

It has not always been the case that the standard of judging has been consistently as high as it is today. Alan Armstrong critiqued the standard of judging at competitions in an article he wrote for *Te Ao Hou* in 1965. Alan, who was a Major in the New Zealand Army, was in charge of the First Battalion Royal New Zealand Infantry Regiment's concert party in 1968 when I was a young officer in Malaysia. Under his tutorship the concert party was an outstanding example of kapa haka. Tragically he died at an early age as he had the experience, knowledge and skills to have made a larger impact on contemporary kapa haka. It was Alan's experience that many competitions were poorly organised and subject to unsatisfactory judging. It was also his view that a clear set of rules was needed so that competitors knew what was expected of them.

These rules must define such points as what each team is expected to perform in the way of items before it can qualify for an aggregate prize (if any), whether original compositions are required, the system of marking, whether any conventions of dress such as moko are mandatory, and whether there is a requirement for any particular type and direction of entrance.

Alan argued that judging is not an exercise in intuition. He observed that the best group is not necessarily the one that 'brings a lump to the throat and raises a laugh':

The judge must be fair to those who have practised long and hard, and not let careless groups cash in merely because they make more noise and get the audience laughing with them and cheering for them. . . . If teams are to get the full benefit from a competition, it is not sufficient merely to be told that they were not placed first. They have a right to be told where they went wrong and where their technique requires improvement. Then they can go away and work on their faults and perhaps comes back next time and win the competition.

Courtesy Te Waka Huia, Photographer Aaron Smale

Te Waka Huia: innovative kapa haka movements!

Finally, Alan, as ever was his wont, suggested a template to be used for marking haka taparahi. The template below demonstrated a consistency and professionalism that he always adopted in his approach to kapa haka.

Stance:	Are feet well apart? Is stance one of relaxed readiness? Check for sagging waists and hunching shoulders.	10 points
Expression:	Deduct for performers grinning. Expression must be fierce and vigilant. Check use of pūkana, pikari, whātero, whakapī.	10 points
Eyes and Head:	Eyes must watch enemy (audience) but may follow hands for significant actions. Deduct for performers who look around or at the ground.	10 points
Actions:	Crisp? Strong? Decisive? Check hands do not flap, have controlled vibration.	10 points
Coordination:	Everyone working as a team? Watch back rows!	10 points
Start and Stop:	Must be crisp and together. All performers must 'hit' words together when they start. Note position of hands on hips.	10 points
Rhythm:	Is it appropriate to the haka? Make sure tempo of words and actions fit.	10 points
Words:	Every member of group must say them (watch lips). Check for clarity. Do they have sufficient volume, considering the number in the group?	10 points
Leadership:	Has leader good control and presence? Are his words clear and correct? Deduct points if he crosses in front of group.	10 points
Grouping:	Arrangements on stage. Have they given themselves plenty of room?	10 points

Changing of the guard

Over the years since 1972 the kapa haka festivals have been dominated by a number of leaders who have been an inimitable part of the biennial competitions. Kīngi Ihaka, Wiremu Parker and others of that ilk have passed on. Bub Wehi has expanded his activities to encompass the establishment of a training school. Pita Sharples has gone into Parliament and has handed over the mantle of his group to his son, Paora, although it is fair to observe that the 'old warrior' cannot resist the temptation to show off his skills as he did in the 2007 Te Matatini Festival.

More recently, a younger group of leaders has emerged who have learned at the feet of the old masters and are now pushing forward to take their place on the stage. Te Whānau-a-Apanui, the winner of the 2005 Te Matatini Festival, is an example. Rikirangi Gage has for

years been the senior male leader of the group. In 2005, while he still performed, he handed the leadership of the group over to Tāmati Waaka. Not only did the group win the overall championship but Tāmati won the male lead prize.

Over the coming years the strength of kapa haka will grow and in so doing it will contribute to the retention of Māori culture. Moreover, it will continue to provide a means of social commentary, a vent for the release of pent-up frustrations, as well as a means for celebration of the great things that are occurring. It is likely that events such as the positive aspects of the treaty settlement process, the ongoing saga of the fisheries distribution debate and the closing of the inequality gaps will be expressed through kapa haka and before audiences of tens of thousands of Māori and the growing band of interested Pākehā New Zealanders.

Mau rākau — haka and skill at arms

The desire of many young Māori taking part in kapa haka competitions to broaden their knowledge and learning to encompass other aspects of Māori traditional practice have seen growing numbers of young Māori attending training schools to learn mau rākau. 'Mau rākau' literally means 'to hold a stick' and refers to skill at arms in weaponry.

In traditional times an integral part of the preparation for war was training in hand-to-hand combat with a variety of weapons including short clubs like the mere, patu and kotiate and longer spear-like weapons like the taiaha and the tewhatewha. The pictures shown earlier in this book show many of these weapons. In recent times the knowledge relating to the various schools of combat and training was in danger of dying out.

About 30 years ago the art of skill at arms was resurrected in Rotorua by Mita Mohi who is of Te Arawa and Ngāti Tūwharetoa ancestry. A well-known authority on Māori culture, Mita established a mau rākau school on Mokoia Island in Lake Rotorua. Over the years he has spread his message through training schools, including the regular annual sessions held on Mokoia Island. In latter years he has taken his programme into prisons. Mau taiaha programmes have been introduced into prisons on the basis that many Māori prisoners will be helped in their rehabilitation through the imposition of physical and mental discipline and an exposure to traditional knowledge and customs.

The All Blacks and 'Ka Mate!'

The haka 'Ka Mate!' has been performed by the All Blacks, correctly or incorrectly, for over 100 years. It is now as much a part of All Black culture and tradition as the silver fern or the name All Blacks. Other national sports representatives, such as rugby league teams and the Tall Blacks basketball team, also perform the haka, as well as school sports teams at various competitions. However, because of their high profile, and the position of rugby as Aotearoa New Zealand's 'national game', it is the All Blacks' haka performances that have attracted the most attention and, more recently, controversy.

Alexander Turnbull Library, 1/2-051869-F

Praying to the God of Victory! All Blacks in the 1920s try a haka.

The haka has come to symbolise the power of the All Blacks and their place in world rugby. In the 1999 and 2003 Rugby World Cups however, and in recent seasons, the invincibility of the All Blacks has been somewhat tarnished. By association, some would say, the potency of the haka has also been diminished. Since the appointment of Graham Henry as coach of the All Blacks after the disastrous 2003 campaign, where the All Blacks wimped out of the World Cup competitions, we are witnessing the rise of the All Blacks' stocks once more. In recent times we have even seen the unthinkable happen, with the All Blacks performing a new haka (see Chapter 11).

There is no doubt that a well-performed haka before a crucial game can still stir the crowd and unsettle the opponents, but there are so many international matches each year that the spectacle appears to have lost some of its sting, and certainly its spontaneity. The All Blacks' haka is still without doubt an evocative performance though. Combined with a receptive crowd, a nervous opponent or a particularly primed side or one with a point to prove, it still arouses the passion of its participants and the spirits of supporters.

When the All Blacks play the Samoan, Tongan or Fijian national sides, their opponents perform their own traditional dances, and the spectacle is greatly enhanced. It brings to mind the traditional process of challenge and response, and the clashing of opponents, each seeking to establish psychological advantage.

The media, both domestic and foreign, have been quick to seize upon the apparent confrontational nature of the haka. The All Blacks themselves have played up this aspect of it at times. During the 1999 Rugby World Cup, held in the United Kingdom, headlines such as 'Fearsome All Blacks Increase Haka Aggression' were all too common. *The Times* reported:

The sight of 15 battle-ready All Blacks thundering through a Haka is set to become even more fearsome as the New Zealanders make some aggressive improvisations for the World Cup.[1]

Taine Randell, All Black captain for the 1999 World Cup, told *The Times* that the All Blacks had been practising new moves to the haka which would involve more aggressive actions and gestures, 'including the slapping of chests instead of thighs at critical points'.[2] Randell suggested that the actions were stronger and would better describe what the All Blacks were about.

Because internationally the haka is synonymous with the All Blacks it is not surprising that foreign companies and journalists seek information about the haka from the New Zealand Rugby Union. When searching the internet with the keyword 'haka', the first website listed is www.haka.co.nz, a site dedicated to the All Blacks and the haka 'Ka Mate!'. When debate erupted over the use of the haka 'Ka Mate!' in a foreign commercial, the production company argued that they had sought advice from the New Zealand Rugby Union on its use.

Debate over All Blacks' use of the haka

In recent years, there has been much debate over the All Blacks' performance of the haka, and whether they should perform it at all. Some ask whether their performance of the haka is still the embodiment of a fearsome challenge or simply a symbolic cultural gesture that no longer has a place in today's professional game.

It is true that, because it is performed so often now, the haka seems to have lost some of its power as a psychological tool of war. If it is just a cultural exhibition then, as some

Taine Randell (centre) leaps high in his leadership of the haka before the All Blacks played France in the semi-final of the World Cup at Twickenham, London, 1999.

suggest, perhaps it would be more relevant to have a cultural group perform it really well. Alternatively, if the haka is a team-building exercise, perhaps it should be relegated to the dressing room before the game.

These questions and observations reflect the changing role of haka in rugby. And just as there is debate among Māori leaders about the place of haka in Māori society, the place of the haka in rugby is likewise debated by its leaders: administrators, commentators, journalists and notable players.

Paul Lewis, writing in the *New Zealand Listener* shortly after the Wales–New Zealand test match in 2006 when the All Blacks refused to perform the haka on the pitch (more on that subject later), suggested that the haka may have had its day:

> It may be a good time to park the haka in the garage and draw the canvas over it. All the bombast over the 'haka strike' at the recent Wales–All Black test match at the Millennium Stadium did little credit to both sides; it merely underlined the fact that the haka simply doesn't fit any more in rugby's increasingly commercialised and political environment.

Lewis lamented the fact that the haka is overexposed and performed too frequently. He opined that it:

> . . . isn't about culture any more. It's about cash. The All Black 'brand' is a powerful and effective tool that puts bums on seats and was the reason the England test was shoehorned into this year's tour itinerary — so both unions could make some money.[3]

Colin Meads, the outstanding rugby player of the twentieth century, was outspoken about wanting to see the haka dropped from All Black games. In 2001, Meads said he could not see the usefulness of the haka in achieving results, and thought that the All Blacks put more passion into the haka than they did into their game. He had felt self-conscious about performing it in his time with the All Blacks, he said.[4]

Meads' views were met with plenty of criticism. An outraged letter writer, H Green, writing to the *Waikato Times*, said:

> My son went overseas with his rugby team and while they were away on the tour this haka thing came up again. When they returned I asked a couple of my son's Pakeha friends what they felt and thought of doing the haka. One guy said it gave him heaps of mana before the game. The other said it made him feel awesome before and after the game . . . this was enough for me. If Colin Meads didn't take part in the haka while he was an All Black, fair enough, but I am disappointed in his comments.[5]

However, former All Black Chris Laidlaw agreed with Meads that the haka was 'undergoing some degree of devaluation'. He thought it would be unwise to not have it, though. Laidlaw thought that the haka and its use was evolving, and noted that it was being performed 'with a good deal more expertise than we used to do it'.[6]

If the place of the haka was coming under challenge from old stalwarts of the game like Colin Meads and the less than convincing performance of the All Blacks, it was in the late 1990s and early 2000s also coming under pressure from those who wished to claim it as a tribal property.

Haka as intellectual property

Over the last decade a debate has raged over who owns the haka 'Ka Mate!'. The increase in temperature around this issue coincided with the All Blacks getting ready to go to Europe in 1999 to contest the Rugby World Cup. It heated up further as the All Blacks recovered from their disastrous 1999 campaign and readied themselves for the next World Cup in 2003. In 2000 Ngāti Toa, Te Rauparaha's tribe, advised the New Zealand Rugby Union that it would be trademarking the famous haka and that they would charge a fee for its use. In the age of professional rugby, international sponsorship and the reputedly large sums top rugby players are paid, it is not surprising that Ngāti Toa would want a slice of the action.

Ngāti Toa, through researcher Oriwa Solomon, applied to register the haka as a trademark, based on the premise that the haka should be protected as identifiable cultural property because it did not belong to everyone. Solomon made it clear that he thought that it should belong to Ngāti Toa.

However, not all Ngāti Toa shared Oriwa Solomon's view about 'Ka Mate!'. Ngāti Toa kaumātua (elder) Puoho Kātene said that the famous haka was a gift from the tribe to the nation and that it did not want any money for it. However, what he did want to do was ensure that the haka could not be exploited for money.[7]

Intellectual property lawyer John Hackett advised that it was impossible to trademark the haka because it could not be distinguished as a product or service in the course of trade. Hackett said the haka would be classified as a song or a challenge, not a trademark. As such, it came under the Copyright Act, but that was also unlikely to apply to the original haka as copyright only existed for 50 years after the composer's death.

In June 2000, Willie Jackson, then a Member of Parliament, and head of the Mana Motuhake political party, criticised the New Zealand Rugby Union for its use of the haka.[8] Jackson welcomed talk of Ngāti Toa charging for the haka. He did not believe other sports were in the same boat, because they did not use Māori images so commercially. 'If all they

Photosport

The New Zealand Māori rugby team perform the haka before their historical win over the British Lions, Waikato Stadium, Hamilton, Saturday, 11 June 2005.

[Ngāti Toa] are going for is $1.5 million, they are selling themselves short,' Jackson said.

New Zealand Rugby Union Chief Executive Officer David Rutherford said the union would consult with Māori if the haka became commercial property, but felt it was unlikely they would pay for the privilege to perform a ritual that had been a part of All Black rugby for over 100 years. He considered that paying for the haka would demean it, and said the rugby union regarded the haka 'as part of the jersey and everything that goes with it'.

At the height of the controversy Dr Charles Royal, an academic at Te Wānanga o Raukawa and an expert on cultural issues, suggested that the rugby union commission their own haka. The response from All Black manager Colonel Andrew Martin was that the All Blacks had no intention of writing another haka, as they already had one!

However, as I observed at the time there was a lot of merit in Dr Royal's suggestion. When the New Zealand Māori rugby team played the Argentinian Pumas in June 2001 they performed a haka especially composed for them, and were supported by fully costumed kapa haka performers.[9]

The New Zealand Māori rugby team' haka begins deep within the creation myth and the evolution of Māori from te kore, the nothingness, to te pō, the dark, and then to the light. It describes the separation of Papatūānuku, the Earth Mother, and Ranginui, the Sky Father, and the creation of human life itself.

The haka then exhorts the young men to aspire to acquire mātauranga (knowledge) and whanaungatanga (unity) and to reach taumatatanga (the pinnacles of excellence). It is a haka with deep symbolism and requires that those who carry it out know what it is they are chanting. Interestingly, the composer has intertwined a truncated version of the sentiments of Robert Browning into the haka: If you aim for the mountains, you will hit the plains!

The All Blacks' management's rejection of Royal's suggestion of a new haka was not the end of the matter. As will be shown in the next chapter, the All Blacks did indeed commission another haka in 2004 and this was revealed in Dunedin in 2005, prior to a test match against the Springboks.

Haka and the tradition of the All Black rugby team

While the haka has over time been immortalised by generations of All Black teams travelling overseas, there is some debate over when a haka was first used as a pre-game ritual.[10] The honour of the first team to perform the haka before a game has long been attributed to a 'Native' team which toured Britain in 1888. The team was made up of mainly Māori players, with four non-Māori.

The team's visit was privately organised and it is suggested that the performance of the haka with the team dressed in traditional costumes might have been a way of defraying the costs of the tour, although the costumes were soon abandoned.

The appearance of the Native team would have caused significant interest amongst British rugby followers. Rugby was still very much a gentleman's game and the thought of a colonial team from the far side of the Empire would have been novel enough. For the team to have mostly Māori players would have piqued the interest of the British even more. The blog site Rugby Pioneers reproduces pictures from the *Illustrated London News* of 13 October 1888 that depict the dress of the Native team, and the response from their opponents and

Courtesy NZ Rugby Museum

The gentlemanly haka! The Originals performing the haka during their tour of Britain 1905–06.

the watching crowd which is typical of the period. An interesting feature is the picture showing the two umpires standing on the field. The Māori umpire is a massive figure with his small tasselled cap atop his head and a cloak draped around his shoulders.[11]

However, a leading sports journalist and rugby author, Spiro Zavos, now living in Australia, claims that the honour for the first overseas team to perform the haka goes to a New Zealand rugby team visiting New South Wales in 1883–84. He quotes a Sydney newspaper to support his case: 'The sound given in good time and union by 18 pairs of powerful lungs was sometimes tremendous'. Not unsurprisingly the Australians thought it inappropriate for '. . . the visitors to frighten them out of their wits before the game began'.

Notwithstanding these early efforts the haka was firmly implanted on the sports field by the 'Originals', the All Blacks who toured Britain in 1905–06. Noted for their dress, their style of play and for the haka, they swept all opponents before them, winning all but one game. Thus was born the fearless reputation of the 'All Blacks', a ruthlessly determined side, which held for much of the twentieth century.

Since the Originals, the haka has been a regular part of the All Blacks' game. However, it would be fair to say that while the All Blacks were highly coordinated and united on the field of play, their efforts at the haka have been somewhat variable over the course of the last 100 years. It was not until the latter part of the twentieth century with leaders like Buck Shelford, that the haka became imbued with the ferocity and unified intensity that comes from practice and an understanding of the words and actions.

How should opposing teams react to the haka?

There has also been debate about what opposing teams should do when witnessing the haka. Up until about 20 years ago, when the All Blacks did the haka, most opposing teams had respectfully stood their distance and watched with a mixture of awe, trepidation and expectation.

The French have typically accepted the haka in their own Gallic way as being one of the necessary preliminary manoeuvres prior to battle. The Australians have tried on occasions, mainly through the media, to upset the All Blacks. In the 1999 World Cup they switched off the sound system. However, these responses are very much muted compared to the reactions of the Home Unions.

In 1989 the Irish national team typically broke ranks with the customary practice — as much to assert their own psychological control of the battlefield as to disrupt the All Blacks' cadence and dominance of the field during the course of the haka. The Irish team faced off with the All Blacks during the haka by moving well forward to challenge them. The Irish rugby captain Willie Anderson did what few rugby players had done and that was to go 'nose-to-nose with Buck Shelford, and survive':

> *In front of a 50,000 capacity crowd as Shelford led the chorus, Anderson's men in green linked arms and began to shuffle forward into the mass of black jerseys. Shelford and Anderson smelt each other's breath as the crescendo of the crowd rose expecting fireworks and a bit of argy-bargy before the game even started. Shelford's eyes were like steel darts; Anderson's arms raised in celebration as he beckoned to the crowd.*[12]

Speaking in an interview in 2001, some 12 years later, the event was obviously still indelibly etched in Anderson's memory. Anderson said that the idea of going head-to-head was hatched up between him and coach Jimmy Davidson before the game started. They wanted to get their supporters behind them. It worked. 'The atmosphere at the game was fantastic.' However, while the Irish might have won the pre-match public relations the All Blacks won the game 23–6.

Anderson said that the All Blacks had extended a challenge and the Irish had accepted it. Shelford himself backed that up and stayed away from any controversy: 'The Haka is a challenge, and they accepted it. It was as simple as that,' said Shelford. 'I certainly did not mind. I suppose it did rile our boys. They played well that day.'[13]

The battle of the hookers! All Black hooker, Norman Hewitt and English hooker, Richard Cockerill face off during the All Black haka, Old Trafford, Manchester, 22 November 1997.

The Newport team in the same year did the opposite and withdrew to behind their goal. Unwittingly they gave the All Blacks the space which was taken and the All Blacks advanced to the 22-metre line to deliver the haka.

Just under a decade later, the English hooker, Richard Cockerill, advanced on the All Blacks and ended up eyeballing his opposite number, Norm Hewitt. A number of observers were horrified that Cockerill should attempt to disrupt the hallowed ritual of the haka. Justin Marshall, the All Black halfback, was quoted, rather naively, as saying: 'It's not meant to be intimidating.'

However, in my view, both Anderson's and Cockerill's actions were perfectly acceptable, and were typical of traditional responses to the haka. When the two famous Māori colleges, Te Aute and St Stephen's, used to meet in their hotly contested rugby matches, the teams would advance on each other, fiercely performing their respective haka in an effort to gain some psychological supremacy.

In recent times the Welsh too have tried their luck. The Welsh are not normally given to psychological games; they normally rely on the powerful singing which erupts out of the valleys and finds its fullest expression during games of rugby, especially when their national team is pitted against the All Blacks.

In 2005 the All Blacks were invited to be a part of the Welsh centenary celebrations of Welsh rugby. As part of the celebrations the All Blacks played the Welsh national team. As a mark of respect for the Welsh the All Blacks agreed to allow the Welsh National Anthem to follow the haka.

The following year, 2006, the Welsh asked the All Blacks to repeat the process. The All Blacks declined, saying that the 2005 event was a one-off. In the week preceding the test match the Welsh Rugby Union, the All Blacks' management and the New Zealand Rugby Union tried to negotiate a solution.

On the day of the match the matter was still unresolved and the All Black players decided, with the support of management and presumably the New Zealand Rugby Union, to not perform the haka on the field. Instead they performed it in their dressing room and so when the All Blacks ran onto the field they had no intention of performing the haka. Instead the haka was shown on the stadium video.

There was stunned silence and then a dawning awareness that the traditional haka would not be performed on the field. There was a growl of disapproval from the crowd. Journalists no doubt relishing the thought of another controversy sharpened their pencils.

All Black lock, Ali Williams, and his team-mates perform the haka for themselves in the dressing room before their match with Wales, Millennium Stadium, Cardiff.

Photosport

Daniel Gilhooly writing for the *New Zealand Herald* from Cardiff on Sunday, 26 November 2006 observed that:

> The All Blacks completed a clean sweep of their European rugby tour in blinding, if controversial, style by sweeping aside Wales 45–10 here today. In an extraordinary break from protocol, the New Zealand players didn't perform their customary haka before kick-off, having done so in the dressing rooms before the teams emerged onto Millennium Stadium. Their action, in response to what they deemed an unreasonable request from the Welsh Rugby Union that the Wales national anthem be the final act before kick-off, was greeted with boos from sections of the 74,000-strong crowd and removed some lustre from another accomplished display.[14]

Wynne Gray, also writing for the *New Zealand Herald*, described it as a PR disaster and observed that:

> This was perhaps the first time overseas that the All Blacks have not performed a haka publicly, and the crowd were not happy. They felt aggrieved that this All Black side, so superior in all respects over Wales, had refused to show its traditional haka. . . . Wales had wanted to change the order of events before the game and had shifted the All Blacks from their usual position — the last act before kick-off. So the All Blacks objected and, apparently, performed their haka in the dressing room. But Wales as host are entitled to run the show. And the All Blacks were far too precious.[15]

Mike Cleary, sports writer for the *Daily Telegraph*, took a poke at the All Blacks on his blog site and advised them to

> Get a life. Don't be so precious. Don't be so sensitive. Sure, big, power-dressed men in black are entitled to come over all touchy-feely and want to preserve their heritage. But not at a test match.

Cleary went on to point out that serious application of the haka did not occur until Buck Shelford became captain of the All Blacks. He argued that before the 1980s the performance of the haka was 'hit and miss'. He thought that since

> Shelford's shrewd stage-management, the haka's importance has become bloated beyond belief. Opposition teams have wasted precious time, as well as grey matter, in working out how to face it. Forget it. Just enjoy it.[16]

Often when occasions like this erupt we tend to default to the defence of our national team instead of considering the relative merits of each side's actions. From a traditional point of view it is perfectly appropriate for the Welsh to seek a response to the haka. Presumably from an All Blacks' point of view there is little merit in giving away the psychological advantage. Whichever way you look at these controversies they tend to give a sharpened edge to the contest itself. And, in any case, the haka has not helped the All Blacks in the last four World Cups and so maybe Cleary is right: we should not take ourselves too seriously!

The All Blacks' new haka – 'Kapa o Pango'

Composing a new haka

In 2004, within the bowels of New Zealand rugby headquarters the unthinkable was taking place. After more than a century of use, the status of 'Ka Mate!' as the sole All Blacks' haka was under review. It is understood that the desire for change was motivated by the senior All Blacks themselves, led by their captain Tana Umaga and embraced by senior management and leading members of the New Zealand Rugby Union.

In truth the furore surrounding the ownership of the haka 'Ka Mate!' must have contributed to an internal discussion around the role of the use of the haka by the All Blacks. Reporter Jon Stokes observed that Robert Solomon, the Chairman of Ngāti Toa:

> *. . . scoffed at claims that the change was driven by copyright claims from descendants of his tribe's ancestral chief Te Rauparaha. 'The All Blacks have used our haka since I was a boy,' he said. 'If they perform a new one that is their choice. We are honoured they have used our taonga for so long.'[1]*

This reaction was in direct contrast to the views held by the tribe some years earlier when the matter of who owned the haka had raged. Whatever the real reason for the change, the New Zealand Rugby Union kept the project under very tight control.

On Saturday, 27 August 2005 the new haka, 'Kapa o Pango', was unleashed onto an unsuspecting New Zealand and world public. The surprise was complete and the launch of the new haka caused immediate controversy. The occasion was the Philips Tri-Nations test against South Africa played in the deep conservative heartland of New Zealand rugby: Carisbrook, Dunedin.

According to the official New Zealand Rugby Union press release announcing the new haka, the All Blacks had learned the haka over the previous year with the intention of expanding the 'All Blacks' tradition of haka' and contributing to the team's heritage.[2] Captain Tana Umaga explained that the team was from many cultures and the use of the haka was one way of bringing them together. Aaron Mauger, another of the All Blacks' old hands and himself part-Māori, observed that the team had reflected over the past year on what it meant to be an All Black 'and the idea for a new haka was one result'. He went on to say:

'Captain Fantastic', Tana Umaga, leads his team in the new haka, 'Kapa o Pango', Carisbrook, Dunedin, 27 August 2005.

We really respect the All Blacks' traditions and the history of 'Ka Mate!'. We felt this group of All Blacks could add to the legacy by writing a haka significant to the All Blacks specifically. 'Kapa o Pango' talks about the silver fern, the blackness of the jersey and living your time as an All Black.[3]

'Kapa o Pango' had been endorsed by the hierarchy of the New Zealand Rugby Union, and its Chairman and former All Black captain Jock Hobbs emphasised the focus on the team when he said:

We all want players to make their mark while they are in the jersey. There's a long All Blacks history that can be daunting. It's critical that every team find a way to contribute to the heritage and not be burdened by it. In addition to its on-field performance, this team has found a respectful way to add to the All Blacks tradition.

'Kapa o Pango' — its immediate impact

The crowd was stunned by the new haka. In particular at the end of the haka the All Black players finished off with a throat-cutting gesture. The furore that followed the game was unprecedented. Pictures of Piri Weepu the All Black halfback with his right thumb being drawn from left to right across his throat flashed around the world.

Jon Stokes of the *New Zealand Herald* observed that:

The throat-cutting gesture at the end of a fierce new All Black haka symbolises the cutting edge of sport and not the slaughter of opponents, says the haka's composer . . . Explaining the gesture, composer and haka expert Derek Lardelli said: 'Playing rugby at this level, with this intensity, is the cutting edge of sport. The players are on the knife edge. They are gladiators in the arena. If they win they are heroes, if they lose they are taken apart.' Mr Lardelli urged understanding of the throat-cutting gesture — performed with particular feeling by halfback Piri Weepu. He said it was symbolic of the intensity of first-class rugby, and the consequences of defeat.

Derek Lardelli — an inspirational composer

Having decided on a course of action to give effect to their internal discussions, the choice of Derek Lardelli by the New Zealand Rugby Union was inspirational. Derek is one of New

Derek Lardelli, composer of 'Kapa o Pango', leads his kapa haka team, Whāngārā-mai-tawhiti, to win the Te Matatini Festival competition, February 2007.

Courtesy of Whāngārā-mai-tawhiti and Te Matatini; Photographer Aaron Smale

Zealand's leading cultural specialists and by naming him to drive through the development of a new haka the New Zealand Rugby Union could not have chosen better.

Derek Lardelli, the man charged with creating a new haka and changing the course of sporting history and tradition is himself a traditionalist. His primary tribal affiliations are to Ngāti Porou on the East Coast and Rongowhakaata and Ngāti Konohi around the Gisborne region. At 46 he is relatively youthful to hold the depth of knowledge of te reo me ōna tikanga (the language and its practice) that he possesses.

Derek is an expert on whaikōrero (speech-making) and he tutors and leads the kapa haka group Whāngārā-mai-tawhiti. In 2007 this group won the fiercely contested biennial Te Matatini kapa haka competition held in Palmerston North. A multi-talented artist in several mediums, including carving, composing and graphic art, he is best known for his tā moko work (the tattooing of traditional Māori designs on the face and other parts of the body). His leadership in the cultural arena is reflected in the many honours already bestowed on him.

He is personable and, notwithstanding his deep knowledge of the lore and traditions of Māori, is not overly prescriptive or fixed in his views and attitudes. These attributes would have seen him fit in well with the All Blacks and the New Zealand Rugby Union as they talked through his challenging assignment.

Inspiration for composing 'Kapa o Pango'

In composing the new haka, Derek turned to his own history and the haka of his ancestors for inspiration. In particular he called on the stirring words of the ancient and famous fighting haka of Ngāti Porou, known and treasured by many generations of Ngāti Porou men, young and old: 'Rūaumoko'. In this haka the imagery and actions are reflective of Rūaumoko, the god of earthquakes and volcanoes. Derek also used elements of another ancient haka 'Te Kiri Ngutu'.

The haka itself is relatively straightforward; the words used are not difficult to articulate and the ideas behind them are simple but powerful. Some haka experts have suggested that it does not have kiko (substance) or body. However, the idea of a haka that can be performed by all has been brilliantly captured by Lardelli. It can be learned relatively easily and will become a hit as it already has among kids at schools. In a short time it will double the repertoire of Aotearoa New Zealanders travelling around the world. Now, as well as 'Ka Mate!' they will have 'Kapa o Pango'.

Subsequent furore around the new haka

The game had barely ended before the media and commentators reacted. The Springbok captain, John Smith, thought it was a compliment to witness the haka for the first time. However, not all commentators were so positive. John Connolly said 'while he has no problem with the traditional Ka Mate haka, he has issues with the Kapa o Pango, introduced by the All Blacks into their pre-match routine last August. "As custodians of the game, we are continually talking about setting an example to young players and throat-slitting probably doesn't send a good message…".'[4]

Sir Howard Morrison responded by telling the media that the Australians should respond with their own haka. He said that he had talked to his nephew Tai McIssac, the Wallaby hooker, and told him that they should lead a response. Sir Howard said that he had called his nephew

Kapa o Pango (All Blacks)

Kapa o Pango kia whakawhenua au i ahau!	Let me become one with the land!

There is a proverb which says that human beings are transitory and land is permanent (toitū te whenua, whatungarongaro te tangata). The idea in this first line seems to be one of linking all members of the team to the substance of Aotearoa.

Hī auē, hī! Ko Aotearoa e ngunguru nei!	This is our land that rumbles!

The imagery in this line captures the essence of the god of volcanoes, Rūaumoko, and indicates this as an integral part of Aotearoa New Zealand. It also suggests the explosive nature of volcanoes and translates this idea into the power of the All Blacks.

Au, au, auē hā!	And it's my time! It's my moment!

Lardelli in his comments places great emphasis on these simple lines. Exploding out of the notion of the volcano god we have an urgent and powerful release of energies. The players are saying, 'We are here. We are the All Blacks. It is our time to perform.'

Ko Kapa o Pango e ngunguru nei!	This defines us as the All Blacks!

The culminating expression of all that goes before is that 'We are the All Blacks!' This line lays down a challenge to the world and says, 'Watch out! We are not to be trifled with!'

Au, au, auē hā!	It's my time! It's my moment!

Again the reinforcement of the players' expression of confidence and self-belief.
Lardelli describes 'hā' as the breath of life.

I āhaha! Ka tū te ihiihi	Our dominance

The next three lines emphasise the All Blacks as a superpower in world rugby and that they are not about to give this pre-eminent position away easily.

Ka tū te wanawana	Our supremacy will triumph
Ki runga ki te rangi e tū iho nei, tū iho nei, hī!	And will be placed on high
Ponga rā!	Silver fern!

In the traditional haka 'Te Kiri Ngutu' from which these lines are taken, Sir Āpirana Ngata translates these words as 'the shadows fall'. Lardelli is literally correct.

Kapa o Pango, auē hī!	All Blacks!
Ponga rā!	Silver fern!
Kapa o Pango, auē hī, hā!	All Blacks!

. . . after the last test and said to him, 'The haka is no more than a challenge. If a challenge is issued, you are to step forward and do the same thing. You have the mana of Te Arawa and are a representative of your people, you do not have to stand there and accept it.' He said Kapa o Pango's throat-slitting gesture was not to be taken literally but was part of the challenge, which should be met with a response.[5]

The Times reacted to the new haka with outrage:

If a crazed thug drew a finger threateningly across his throat while screaming into someone's face on a high street, police would have good grounds for arrest. Why should such antics be tolerated on a rugby field two minutes before kick-off?[6]

David Farrar, the quintessential Kiwi blogger, took a poke at *The Times* reaction, observing that such comments only served to convince him that there should be no changes to the new haka, noting: 'Anything which riles the Poms this badly has to be great.'[7]

Support for the new haka came from many quarters. Tim Groser, the National Party spokesman on Arts, Culture and Heritage, in a speech on 28 November 2006 observed:

If you had asked me whether I would consider it a 'good thing' if the traditional Te Rauparaha haka should, at least on occasions, be replaced by a new haka, I am certain I would have replied with a defiant 'no'. I suspect the vast majority of New Zealanders would have given the same conservative reply. But when I saw, for the first time, the new

Piri Weepu (left), All Black halfback, demonstrates the controversial slitting action across his throat at the Tri-Nations and Bledisloe Cup match between the All Blacks and Australia, Jade Stadium, Christchurch, 8 July 2006.

haka 'Kapa o Pango' unveiled against the South Africans at Carisbrook in 2005, my jaw literally dropped. It was simply stunning. It was a rare moment when suddenly various cultural currents came together as a result of the genius of the author of the new haka and the passion of our players. Our differences were there on show, but the unity it produced was uplifting.[8]

The Far North District Mayor, Yvonne Sharp, writing in her mayor's column in the *Northern Age* on 1 September 2006 took the opportunity to comment on the new haka:

On Saturday night, the All Blacks unleashed the new haka, 'Kapa o Pango', before playing and beating the Springboks — and the nation responded. Like many other New Zealanders I watched the rugby game on Saturday evening . . . Our international games have always been kicked off with a stirring haka, reflecting our sense of pride in being New Zealanders. The new haka on Saturday, 'Kapa o Pango', took us one important step forward as a nation.

Even that redoubtable All Black legend, Colin Meads, who in 2001 called for the banning of the haka from the All Blacks arsenal, came out in praise of the new haka! '[He] applauded the change and said he believed it had helped to inspire the All Blacks and the crowd.'[9]

Review of 'Kapa o Pango' by NZRU

Almost a year after the controversial launch of 'Kapa o Pango' the New Zealand Rugby Union released the results of its review of the new haka. The principal finding was that the broader public needed to have a greater understanding of haka. The rugby union had also sought a more in-depth explanation from Derek Lardelli about the throat-slashing action that had led to so much controversy.

The New Zealand Rugby Union commissioned pollsters Colmar Brunton to assess the views of New Zealanders on 'Kapa o Pango'. The company polled 500 New Zealanders. The results of the research released by the rugby union reflected an overwhelming support for the All Blacks doing the haka (88%). A significant proportion of those polled (62%) had a positive view about the new haka. A similar percentage of those polled (60%) thought either haka was appropriate to be performed before test matches.

When it came to views about the appropriateness of the final throat-slashing gesture of 'Kapa o Pango', opinion was more divided: 47% thought the haka should be left untouched, while 37% thought the final gesture should be removed. These results would have been pleasing to the NZRU as they reflected a sense that the majority of New Zealanders understood and appreciated the place of haka in rugby tradition.

In the NZRU's media release of 8 July 2006 Lardelli clarified the meaning of the word 'hā' and the actions of the right arm in the final gesture of the haka. His explanation is that '"Kapa o Pango" ends with the word "Ha" which translates as the breath of life. The words and motions represent drawing vital energy into the heart and lungs.' The right arm searches for the 'Ha' on the left side of the body, Lardelli explained, while the head turns to the right, also symbolically seeking vital energy. The right hand hauls that energy into the pouwhakaora (the heart, lungs and air passages), then the eyes and tongue signal that the energy has been harnessed before it is expelled with the final 'Ha'.

'Kapa o Pango' — Lardelli responds

As part of its orchestrated response, the NZRU posted a video featuring Derek Lardelli on the All Blacks site that sought to provide further explanation of the meaning of the haka 'Kapa o Pango', including the meaning of the final gesture and the difference between 'Kapa o Pango' and 'Ka Mate!'. Lardelli was supported in the official explanation by Keven Mealamu and Aaron Mauger. All three sang in unison off the same song sheet — which is not a surprise. The full transcript is set out below:

What does 'Kapa o Pango' mean?

Derek Lardelli: *'Kapa o Pango' is fundamentally what we call haka taparahi — it's ceremonial, it's about building spiritual, physical and intellectual capacity prior to doing something very important.*

There are hakas that use weapons — peruperu; those types of hakas, they are war hakas, but this haka in particular is not a war dance, it's ceremonial, it's about building the person's confidence inwardly; their spiritual side and making that spiritual side connect through the soul and coming out through the eyes, the hands and the gestures, so it's a preparation of your physical side as well as your spiritual side.

Keven Mealamu: *I personally think we are doing it for ourselves; for us as individuals as well. Personal meaning behind it — for us it's something which helps us prepare for our game. For us it's not a war dance but ceremonial . . . So for me it just helps me prepare for the game.*

Derek Lardelli: *'Kapa o Pango' is about a group of young men that wanted to express themselves during haka and my job was to compose, to put actions to that particular expression. It's about them. Ko au, au, auē hā! It talks about — this is my time in the black jersey; this is my time to express myself as a player on behalf of my country. And because they'd done 'Ka Mate!' so well it was an obvious progression for them to move into creating something that would be part of their legacy for other players when they came through.*

What about the concerns about the final gesture of 'Kapa o Pango'?

Aaron Mauger: *There's been a lot of misinterpretation I think about the haka in the last year or so. We probably haven't been the best at explaining it ourselves — the European interpretation which was put across last year was the cutting edge!*

The Māori translation for us — the breath of life; the hā means the breath of life. This action here [in the video Mauger describes the action of his right hand sweeping from near the top left-hand side of his neck, diagonally and down to the right across the trunk of his body covering the area of his vital organs], the bringing it across the body is energising the vital organs; the heart, the lungs, all those things we need to be functioning well for the game . . . that's what that means; getting that energy back into the system before we start our game.

Derek Lardelli: *Haka is about challenging peoples' perspectives. But if we look at that particular action again we cannot say that it is only one action. It must be connected to the whole haka because then you see the meaning behind it. When the players get to that*

stage in the haka their legs are burning; they are gasping for air. The action is actually to grab a hold of the energy that exists on the left and haul it through those vital organs: your heart, your lungs and . . . your air passages and grasp that energy; and then let it go and expel that whole delivery so that you have revitalised yourself for the game.

Aaron Mauger: *It's for the players really. For the modern All Blacks it's about time in the jersey, the silver fern and the blackness of the jersey and those sorts of things that are relevant to the All Blacks.*

How do 'Ka Mate!' and 'Kapa o Pango' relate to each other?

Aaron Mauger: *It is certainly not there to replace 'Ka Mate!'. It is there as a brother alongside it, so we are pretty proud of 'Ka Mate!' as well, we will use both as passionately as each other.*

Derek Lardelli: *'Ka Mate!' is the foundation haka that the All Blacks have always used. The new haka, 'Kapa o Pango', is but part of another dimension that we wish to add to and help 'Kapa o Pango' and 'Ka Mate!' come together. 'Ka Mate!' is the tuakana, the older brother. 'Kapa o Pango' is the younger brother. We are building a family of haka here. It is about helping the dimension of haka in the All Blacks. They do it well.*

Whatever the explanation we now have another powerful haka in the arsenal of not only the All Blacks but also all Aotearoa New Zealanders. A heartening sign of progress was that a number of leaders in the All Blacks including a Samoan (Tana Umaga), a Pākehā (Richie McCaw) and of course Piri Weepu and Rico Gear can step up and lead. This All Black team's execution of the haka is the most polished of any All Black team yet.

All Blacks perform the haka 'Kapa o Pango' prior to the test match between New Zealand and France, Eden Park, Auckland, 2 June 2007.

12 Other sports and haka

Over the years Aotearoa New Zealand national teams have taken their lead from the All Blacks in two respects. Firstly there is a prevalence of the word 'black' in the team name. Our national cricket team is called the Black Caps. The national hockey team is called the Black Sticks. The men's basketball team is called the Tall Blacks. And, secondly, there has been a tendency to use the haka 'Ka Mate!' as the team haka.

Given that these are national teams with finely tuned athletes, it is not surprising that they quickly adapt to and embrace symbols of their nation which they can project with pride. As much as anything, it's an expression of pride in being at the pinnacle of their chosen sport. The haka has become an obvious vehicle for teams to collectively express their will in front of their supporters.

Aotearoa New Zealand
Olympic and Commonwealth games teams

In some national teams the wish to embrace the haka has been limited to its performance and not necessarily at a high level of excellence. However, in recent times normally conservative sports teams have made the decision to go beyond the haka itself, to understand its cultural significance and to understand the context from which it derives.

A good example of this approach is seen with the New Zealand Olympic Committee, which has responsibility for managing both the Olympic and Commonwealth games teams. Under the broad direction of the New Zealand Olympic Committee and the specific leadership of Dave Currie, Chef de Mission of the New Zealand Olympic Team, a major effort was made to incorporate Māori culture into the team's preparation for the Athens Olympics in 2004 and subsequently the 2006 Commonwealth Games in Melbourne.

The New Zealand Olympic Committee approached the Sports and Recreation Council (SPARC) to facilitate the incorporation of Māori cultural elements into the Aotearoa New Zealand team's preparation for the Athens Olympics. The Chief Executive Officer of SPARC, Nick Hill, in a press release commending the leadership of the New Zealand Olympic Team in reflecting the unique identiy of Aotearoa New Zealand, said:

> This initiative is just one of many that have been developed in a growing relationship between SPARC and the NZOC leading up to the Athens Games beginning in August. We commend the NZOC for embracing Maori culture and making it an integral part of the team's sporting identity. It provides an amazing backdrop for our athletes to perform in the high pressure environment of the Olympic Games and celebrates who we are as a nation.[1]

Pivotal to the development of the changes envisaged was the Māori Advisory Committee to the NZOC comprising Amster Reedy, subsequently appointed as Cultural Advisor to the team; Waana Davis, Chair of Toi Māori, a charitable trust with the objective of fostering the development of Māori arts; and Trevor Shailer, of the Health Sponsorship Council.

The close relationship that developed between Chef de Mission Dave Currie and Amster Reedy enabled Reedy to quickly get athletes and administrators on board. Reedy provided the cultural context for the team and not only taught the athletes haka but also explained the reasons why certain actions took place. He introduced karakia (prayer) and other aspects of Māori culture into the lives of the athletes.

The impact of the new approach was immediately evident in Athens, with the athletes embracing the performance of haka within the Aotearoa New Zealand village. Athletes from a diverse range of sports performed the haka before they started events and as a celebration of victory. Bevan Docherty, who won a silver medal in the triathlon, said that:

> The medal ceremony was amazing, what an honour to have your national anthem played at the biggest sporting event in history, and to have Mum, Dad and Fee there was truly special. . . . However the most touching thing was coming back to the Olympic village, to be welcomed by the entire NZ Olympic team as they did the Haka, it truly sent shivers down my spine.[2]

117

Reedy accompanied the Olympic team to Athens in 2004, the Winter Olympics in Italy in 2006 and to the Commonwealth Games in Melbourne in 2006, where the concept was expanded. The sight of the Aotearoa New Zealand Sevens Rugby team doing the haka was inspirational to its legions of fans. The energy and the passion, perfectly synchronised, was projected across our TV screens into our living rooms and it was as if we were there with them!

The Tall Blacks

The Aotearoa New Zealand men's basketball team has over the years had a patchy history of success, often playing second fiddle to trans-Tasman rivals Australia. In 2001 the team played out of their skins and surprised the basketball world by defeating the Australian Boomers to qualify for the 2002 World Championships.

At this time the team would perform a pre-match haka led by Brendon Pongia, who was not a team member but was specifically there to lead the haka. At the World Cup the supporters were often charged up and from time to time vented their enthusiasm with a haka from the stands.

The Tall Blacks became quite a talking point at the championships. Because of their minnow status, their unlikely entry to the World Championships at the expense of the Australian Boomers was meritorious enough, without them doing anything else. On top of this their great success in coming fourth at the World Championships was an extraordinary feat.

The other reason for the Tall Blacks attracting international media attention was their performance of the haka before their games. *Sports Illustrated* senior writer Alexander Wolff, writing under the headline 'Thunder Down Under', described the impact of the haka on the opposing teams:

> *The Tall Blacks perform the haka, a traditional Maori dance, before every game. Think of those defensive slide drills you see at Five Star only with chanting and gesticulation. The haka is both a sign of respect for your opponent and an expression of your own determination to meet a challenge. The New Zealanders expect opponents to look on politely, but the Russians turned their backs and the Venezuelans derisively imitated the haka's movements, infuriating their American coach, Jim Calvin, who had warned his players not to let the haka get into their heads. 'They misunderstood,' Cameron, one of four Tall Blacks of Maori descent, said of the Venezuelans. 'It's just to prepare us to go into battle, to do what it takes.'*[3]

Pero Cameron leads the New Zealand Tall Blacks in a haka before playing the Czech Republic, Mystery Creek, Hamilton, 10 July 2003.

Photosport

In reviewing the photo galleries and the various blog sites regarding the Tall Blacks and the haka it is clear that the Tall Blacks have a long way to go before they can match the benchmark of excellence set by the All Blacks. Nevertheless, if the haka can help them prepare for the combative nature of the fierce competitions they take part in it makes sense for them to improve their performance in it!

The Kiwis

The Kiwis rugby league team has always been the poor second cousin to the All Black rugby team. Nevertheless the game is played between the three strong rugby league nations: Australia whose team is called the Kangaroos; the British team whose team is called Great Britain or the Lions; and the Aotearoa New Zealand team which is called the the Kiwis.

In the past the haka has not been a significant or frequent feature of pre-game ceremonies before the Kiwis played the other major league nations. In 1958 the Kiwis rugby league team did perform haka before tests with the Great Britain Lions. It is clear from the photograph of the haka ceremony prior to one of their games that the players are not as experienced at the haka, as most of them seem to be trying to fly!

In recent years the Kiwis have tended to use the haka more frequently. The Kiwis rugby league management in 2006 moved formally to appoint a cultural advisor, Bailey Mackey, to improve players' understanding and performance of the haka.

Photosport

Redoubtable warrior, Ruben Wiki, captain of the Kiwis rugby league team leads them in a haka before they played Great Britain in the Gillette Tri-Nations series, Westpac Stadium, Wellington, 11 November 2006.

With a growing number of Kiwis players born outside New Zealand, the NZRL decided to engage Mackey before the Tri-Nations to help give them a greater understanding of the history and traditions associated with the team.

Prior to the October 2006 test between the Kangaroos and the Kiwis, Mackey addressed the players about the importance of the haka.

The Kiwi, our national bird, the fern, our national plant, the black and white V, our national colours, and the haka are things that make New Zealand sporting teams unique on the international stage.

The *Sydney Morning Herald* of 21 October 2006 reported that a number of Māori elders and ex-Kiwi League players at the game reckoned the haka performed by the Kiwi League Team was the best seen in '100 seasons'.[4] However, not all watchers were impressed with the haka. The antics of opposition teams trying to diminish the haka is not only restricted to teams playing the All Blacks. Playing in the Australian team was Willie Mason, the giant second-rower of part-Māori ancestry. While the Kiwis performed their haka, Mason mouthed off obscenities. Soon after the game started he was mauled by the Kiwis and got up after a brutal tackle by David Kidwell sporting a very swollen black eye.

Mason, never one to back off from a scrap, later claimed in a newspaper column that he was not being disrespectful:

I suppose everyone wants to know why I swore during the haka before Saturday's Test match in Auckland. I'll tell you why and it has nothing to do with disrespecting New Zealand. I was actually standing next to Justin Hodges during the haka and I said to him, 'Isn't Brent Webb an Aborigine? Look at him. Get f---ed' . . . I certainly wasn't disrespecting the haka or the Māori culture because I think it's one of the highlights of both international rugby league and rugby union matches. I look forward to the Kiwis doing the haka . . . But seriously, what do they expect us to do? Bloody crawl into a hole while they're doing it? We've got to do something. That's why we all stood there to show them how united and tight that we are as a team.[5]

Mackey's subsequent riposte to Mason's complaint about an Australian, Brent Webb, not only playing for the Kiwis but performing the haka was that:

Players from other teams, like Willie Mason, can't perform the haka, so it's a privilege and an honour to those that don the black and white 'V', the Kiwi and the fern, and that includes our Torres Strait Island brother, Brent Webb, our Queensland brother, Nathan Fien, and anyone else — because once you don the black and white jersey, you're part of the brotherhood.[6]

Haka and politics

From the early twentieth century, the haka has been part of the ceremony and drama of political protest, becoming a vehicle through which Māori have expressed their frustrations at the laws of successive governments, both national and local, and as a rallying cry for their causes.

During the 1995 protests by Māori against the National Government's treaty settlement policies, groups used haka to give full vent to their frustration or opposition. The haka performed at various meetings were often quite frightening in their vehemence and passion, and became symbols of rejection of the Government's policies, loudly signalling anger and disillusionment. Protesters left no doubt among officials and ministers of the Crown that Māori were not happy!

In some ways, the use of haka in political protest and the debate surrounding its use and misuse, including its growing acceptance by non-Māori as a national icon, are examples of how the haka provides a mirror of the ongoing debate and dialogue between Māori and Pākehā in Aotearoa New Zealand in general. The haka will no doubt continue to be used to focus attention on issues affecting Māori, and to show the measure of their feelings when making political protests.

The 'haka incident'

Some of the incidents surrounding haka also provide a gauge of progress or lack of it in race relations. A well-known incident that perhaps best exemplifies the potential tensions surrounding the misuse of the haka occurred in 1979, when a group of Pākehā engineering students at Auckland University were forced to stop their parody of the haka, an event that had been a capping week stunt for many years.

Just before 10am on the morning of 1 May 1979 a group of 20 or so Māori and Pacific Islanders confronted the engineering students during a rehearsal of their 'haka' in the engineering faculty's common room. The raid lasted just a few minutes, during which the engineering students were told not to mock Māori culture and some had their fake grass skirts ripped from their bodies. There was then an exchange of blows between the attackers and the engineering students, which left many of the students with cuts and bruises, and three with more serious injuries.

Race relation conciliators, Pita Sharples (left), the late Harry Dansey (middle), at Auckland University wait to address students in 1979, following the confrontation between Māori and Pacific Island protesters and engineering students.

The mock haka had been part of capping week activities since 1954. Authorities and police had tolerated it as part of the helter-skelter activities expected immediately prior to and during capping week.

Māori, on the other hand, had over the years objected to the practice as an insult to the culture. According to researcher Kayleen Haselhurst:

Maori objections increased as the engineering students took more and more licence with the mock ceremony and daubed themselves with obscene sexual symbols and used offensive phrases and gestures . . .[1]

One of the offensive phrases, which would have made most Māori seethe with anger, went as follows:

Ka mate! Ka mate! (stamping feet and slapping thighs)
Hōri! Hōri! (left hand patting the head, right hand simulating masturbation)
I got the pox from
Hōri! Hōri! (Hōri, meaning 'George', has long been used as a derogatory term for Māori.)[2]

The aftermath of this incident says much about the attitudes of the time. In the media the attackers were pilloried, with very few reports attempting to look at the issues surrounding the incident. Among the Māori group were Hone Harawira and Ben Dalton, two outspoken men from the north of Aotearoa New Zealand. Dalton's evidence indicated that he had taken part in the incident because he felt that

. . . all other avenues to make the students desist in making fun of our culture have failed. I have been trying to make representations through the students for three or four years. Those have failed so we tried a personal approach today. I wanted passive resistance and so did others with me.[3]

The media used terms such as 'gang-related violence', which were bound to incite fear and disapproval among the public, rather than focusing on the issue of the abuse of Māori language and culture.

Māori leaders themselves were not immune from this process. Academics Dr Ranginui Walker and Dr Pat Hohepa led the charge against the gang conspiracy theory and tried to focus attention on the underlying causes of the incident. Their cause was not helped by the Chairman of the New Zealand Māori Council Graham Latimer, who denounced the actions of the Māori group, saying:

The violence in the confrontation between a Maori group and engineering students of Auckland University could not be tolerated in any way at all . . . If we have reached the stage where we cannot grin and bear a little bit of devilment, we have reached a very sorry state.[4]

This view was also held by the Hon. Ben Couch, Minister of Māori Affairs.

However, Latimer's opposition did not last too long as, in the face of a revolt from within the ranks of the powerful New Zealand Māori Council, led by its Auckland affiliate, he was persuaded to change his stance to support the 'principle of protest' of the Māori attackers.

Haka expert and politician — Dr Pita Sharples

Dr Pita Sharples, the parliamentary co-leader of the Māori Party, is a primary example of the warrior tradition. His rise to fame is matched by his growth in the area of haka and its full expression through his various activities over the past four decades.

Born into the Ngāti Kahungunu tribe in the Hawke's Bay, his early schooling days were not particularly auspicious. His knowledge of te reo me ōna tikanga (language and its practice) was not especially strong. However, from his high school days at Te Aute College he became imbued with a strong desire to learn and communicate in the language of his ancestors and to learn the skills that made them feared in hand-to-hand combat. He overcame his limited early knowledge to become one of New Zealand's leading exponents of the haka and lead his Auckland group, Te Roopu Manutaki, to twice win the prestigious national kapa haka festival competitions.

Pita's education at Te Aute College and then Auckland University, where he completed his doctorate in anthropology and linguistics, laid the platform for his rise to prominence, both as a theoretician and also as a practitioner of education. He was a pioneer in the kura kaupapa and kura tuarua movements. Throughout these many years Pita developed his group, Te Roopu Manutaki.

With his characteristic long hair tied in a knot, over the years he has created an image of a taiaha-wielding warrior prepared to stand up for what he believes in and prepared to lead from the front. He has long held strong political views about the need for Māori representation at the highest level.

Sharples was catapulted into the sitting rooms of Aotearoa New Zealanders through his leadership of the massive march to Wellington to protest against the Government's Foreshore and Seabed Bill. Wrapped in a flax cloak, his relatively supple prancing at the head of the protest march, even though he was in his early sixties, left an indelible image of determination and a readiness to stand up for his beliefs.

Dr Pita Sharples (centre) leads the massive Foreshore and Seabed protest to Parliament on 5 May 2004.

While Sharples has handed the reins of leadership in a number of cultural roles to his son Paora, his presence at the recent Te Matatini kapa haka competitions was unmistakable. The *New Zealand Herald* published a vintage photograph of Sharples stripped for action wielding a taiaha. Even at his age he projects all of the signs of leadership one has come to expect of him.

Treaty settlements — Tame Iti

The contemporary use of elements of the haka, including facial contortions, protruding tongue, vigorous limb actions and dramatic gestures, are all part of the make-up of one of New Zealand's best-known protesters, Tame Iti of Tūhoe. Tame is an exponent of the haka and is fond of practising the traditions of his adopted ancestors. Of stocky build he wears a full-facial moko.

Tame Iti was born in Rotorua and brought up by his whāngai (adopted) grandparents in Rūātoki, a small village near Whakatāne in the eastern Bay of Plenty. From an early age he was an activist and his political leanings have over the years been eclectic. As a member of the Communist Party he went to China in 1973. During the Māori renaissance of the 1970s and 1980s Tame Iti was never far from the action.[5]

Over the years Tame Iti's protest actions have included baring his buttocks, spitting at dignitaries being welcomed onto the Treaty Grounds at Waitangi, standing in the Rangitāiki River to halt the progress of a jet-boat race and setting up a Māori Embassy on Parliament grounds.

On 6 January 2005, Tame Iti took part in one of the most dramatic replications of history in modern times.

It was a Sunday and Tūhoe had gathered in their hundreds to welcome a group of visiting Waitangi Tribunal members and lawyers to the Rūātoki area, to begin hearings on the Tūhoe claim, that was based on Tūhoe allegations that the Government had illegally seized its lands in the mid-nineteenth century. The Tūhoe people are known as 'the children of the mist', a name that derives from their home in the mountains of the Urewera. They have a distinctive dialect which includes pronouncing 'ng' as 'n' and the strength of their language is unmatched by most other tribes.

The Crown representatives were asked to assemble on the confiscation line, the boundary of the land confiscated by the Crown in the 1860s, which is for Tūhoe, a mark of the shame which befell them when the Crown took their land.

The Crown party waited for a buggy to carry the judge and senior officials to the marae where the serried ranks of Tūhoe were waiting to greet them. Indigimedia, which has a pro-Māori focus, reported on the events:

Tame Iti, Tuhoe activist.

Getty

A young Tuhoe tribesman, tino rangatiratanga flag in hand, riding a horse bareback, gallops down the valley to where the Crown is waiting . . . Dozens of Tuhoe on horses follow behind him. The Crown is carried by horse-drawn cart across the 'aukati line' or confiscation line toward Tauarau Marae at Ruatoki; they are greeted by 600 chanting Tuhoe. Those on horseback have begun a tirade of insults and curses.

The Crown party, by now alerted to the intensity and height of emotions being expressed, moved with some trepidation down the road towards Tauarau marae amid the shouting and constant movement of horses and people. After the horsemen, they were greeted with vehicles that had been placed 100 metres apart on alternate sides of the road. Between the cars were bonfires. The smoke and flames added dramatic theatre to the already tension-charged atmosphere. According to Indigimedia's reporter, the cars 'symbolise a re-enactment of when the Crown practised a scorched earth policy in the area during the 1860s. A policy which saw an invasion of Tuhoe where many were killed, exiled, arrested, with villages razed to the ground.'

When the Crown party reached the confiscation line they were met with

. . . Kaiwero-challengers . . . gathered at the confiscation line smeared with mud, many of these naked male warriors and semi-naked warrior women are adorned with ta-moko. Gunshots reverberate around the gathering, adding to the atmosphere of this highly charged crowd. Manawa-wera and other types of haka also boom down the Ruatoki valley from the confiscation line.

Tame took part in a haka welcome to the visitors. Naked except for a small hat perched on his head and a blanket wrapped around himself and carrying a double-barrelled shotgun he advanced forward of the front of the ranks of assembled Tūhoe men and women. He then discharged his weapon into a New Zealand flag, scaring the wits out of the visiting delegation.

Iti explained that he wanted to replicate the anxiety and fear from the land wars of the 1860s: 'We wanted them to feel the heat and smoke, and Tūhoe outrage and disgust at the way we have been treated for 200 years.'[6]

While the incident was filmed and shown on national television there was no reaction from the police. It was not until the matter was raised in Parliament that the police acted and charged Tame for unlawful possession of a firearm. In June 2006 he defended himself in Māori and was found guilty of the unlawful possession of a firearm in a public place. This conviction was quashed by the Court of Appeal in April 2007.

This series of events, the colourful expressions and dress, and not least of all the haka, were a metaphor for the way in which Tūhoe felt about the Crown and about the confiscation of 200,000 acres of their land. The use of haka as a living instrument was perhaps best summarised by Iri Akarana-Rewi who said:

Māori culture has lost something, it has become catalogued and contained on performance stages at kapa haka festivals. Tuhoe have taken it off the stage and used it to challenge the powers that be and here it is where it should be in all its honest intensity, in the valleys, on the roads and streets a functioning part of everyday life. My uncle once said that the struggle of people against power was the same as the struggle of remembering against forgetting. Today Tuhoe has chosen not to forget, today Tuhoe has shown us the way.[7]

Haka and bad taste

It is said that one person's treasure is another's kitsch! When it comes to stories about the use of haka postures to illustrate commercial ventures the list and activity seems to be endless. Over the years I can recall a number of occasions when businesses have got into trouble by just assuming they could use Māori legends, famous figures and concepts to sell their products.

One company contemplated the idea of putting the heads of chiefs on tea towels as tourist products. The uproar was considerable. The head is the most tapu (sacred) part of the body, and the head of a chief is particularly tapu. In pre-European times senior chiefs were so tapu they were not allowed to come into direct contact with items that would diminish their sacred status. Food was one of these items. Chiefs were fed by others. Thus the idea of a chief's head on a tea towel was too horrible to think about!

The story below, compiled from a number of sources,[1] is another example of what can happen if full and proper consultation does not take place.

New Zealand Post — the Māori Performing Arts stamp issue

In 2006 New Zealand Post, as part of its role to provide innovative designs reflecting New Zealand culture on its stamps, had set out to promote kapa haka. To this end it had commissioned a designer to come up with designs for five new stamps. The designer developed a number of figures for the stamps depicting various kapa haka postures using both men and women characters.

It was not long after they had sent out a number of packs of stamps to dealers that the new designs ran into trouble. The resistance to the stamp designs was significant, especially from a number of powerful players in the stamp-collecting and dealing fraternity. Well-

The New Zealand Post stamp debacle! Examples of the proposed stamps to celebrate kapa haka withdrawn from sale.

known Rotorua stamp collector and dealer Don Ion led the charge against the new issue describing them as 'insensitive'. Anaru Rangiheua, Chairman of the Te Arawa Trust Board, agreed, describing the designs as 'stupid and insensitive'. He said:

> I don't think Maori should be portrayed like that . . . Even the colours are all wrong. They are modern hand-drawn and not symbolic of Maori. They look cheap and ugly. They should be proper photographs. Maybe they could have taken photos of different marae, with the permission of the tribe, or proper cultural performers, not stupid comic strips.

On 2 June the Chief Executive of New Zealand Post, John Allen, issued a press release advising that New Zealand Post had decided not to release the Māori Performing Arts stamp issue. He stated that the decision followed consultation with a range of people within the Māori arts and culture community, and that concerns about the design style of the stamps had been raised.

The co-leader of the Māori Party, Dr Pita Sharples, applauded the decision by New Zealand Post to withdraw the stamps. In a press release dated 2 June 2006, Sharples was reported as saying:

> Well done, NZ Post, for consulting with tangata whenua — and then actually listening to what Maori said rather than running roughshod over the very people they are looking to honour. . . . New Zealand Post has demonstrated its credibility and professionalism as an organisation, in being prepared to change as a result of adverse feedback.

However, not all Māori opposed the stamp design. Rotorua Deputy Mayor Horowaewae (Trevor) Maxwell expressed regret that the stamps had been withdrawn. He argued that the presentation packs sold with the stamp series would have achieved the objective of promoting kapa haka.

The exercise was a costly one for New Zealand Post. It had to scrap more than one million stamps and the aborted project had cost them about $190,000. However, they had learned from the experience. Chief Executive John Allen said that '. . . New Zealand Post would in the future create a stamp issue that celebrates kapa haka differently'. He also assured the Māori community that they would be 'widely consulted regarding any future stamp series depicting Māori'.

The Canterbury women's rugby team

Another recent example of haka used in a context that many would say was inappropriate was the actions of the Canterbury women's rugby team in England who, to raise funds for their club, were photographed for a calendar bare from the waist up in various haka postures. There was the predictable uproar from haka experts in New Zealand. Some described the actions as scurrilous while others bemusedly shook their heads. The upshot of course was that the team apologised and at the same time probably sold out of their calendars in record time.

Following the subsequent uproar in Aotearoa New Zealand the team apologised and said that they had not intended to upset anyone. Team organiser Rebecca Willis said they had produced 500 copies and they intended to spend the money raised on kit for the team and for the charity Breast Cancer Care.

The reaction in Aotearoa New Zealand was somewhat muted.

Dr Pita Sharples was his usual balanced self, managing to send them a cautionary note but at the same time encouraging them for their effort! He said that he had 'no problem' with the Kent team's fundraising efforts in the UK. But he said the haka was 'a serious thing' in New Zealand. 'Some Maoris were upset by it, not terribly upset, but they thought it was in bad taste', the Māori Party MP added. 'When the club comes to New Zealand, I would expect them to respect the haka. But over there, as a fundraising effort, I wish them well.'[2]

Dr Poia Rewi, senior lecturer in the School of Māori, Pacific and Indigenous Studies at Otago University, said: 'It looks like misuse of the haka to me. . . . I think Māori would be offended by this.' He went on to say:

Women traditionally did do the haka, and if they really wanted to vent their spleen they might have been prompted to expose their private parts. But that's the ultimate expression of soul feeling. If Maori aren't doing it now then I think other people who the culture doesn't belong to should be a bit cautious. It's not something I would promote.[3]

On the one hand he says that traditionally Māori women could haka and express their spleen; but because they don't do that now it should not be done at all! The real issue is why Māori women have been proscribed from actions they used to carry out in traditional times.

There have been a number of other similar examples of misappropriation of the haka. If nothing else these incidents reveal just how much the influence of the haka has spread around the world.

Haka and the global village

It is often said that, as a nation, we can appreciate ourselves better if we see ourselves through others' eyes and through events outside of Aotearoa New Zealand. The growing impact of the haka on our national consciousness is best gauged by the way in which the world views the haka and the way in which Aotearoa New Zealanders use the haka when overseas.

In recent years, there has been increasing attention focused on haka overseas, with some interesting incidents. In 1997, two less than sober Aotearoa New Zealanders were shown on television trying to teach the haka to British pop group the Spice Girls. The group, who were on holiday in Bali, performed their imitation of the haka. This harmless incident caused a furore among senior Māori in Aotearoa New Zealand.

As the world's horizons are reduced through the internet and international travel, we are seeing national symbols and artwork copied or used in a variety of ways overseas. In 2001 New Zealand's High Commissioner to London, Paul East, was among over 100 complainants to the British Independent Television Commission about the screening of an alcohol advertisement in which women with scanty clothing performed the haka. East described the advertisement as offensive and racist. The advertisement, which promoted alcohol-pop fruit drink Reef:

> . . . showed eight women of various nationalities clad only in bikinis and sarongs doing the treasured Maori war dance.[1]

In a follow-up article, the *Dominion* captured the Māori reaction to the British brewery advertisement. Haka specialist Dr Pita Sharples was not concerned about the performance and thought it was a bit of fun which used only elements of the haka. He said he was more concerned that British pop singer Robbie Williams 'has my intellectual property on his shoulder'.[2] He was referring to Williams' tattoo, the work of Māori artist Te Rangitū Netana.

Because there are tens of thousands of Māori living overseas, especially in Australia, it is no surprise that the haka is regularly performed in foreign locations. It was even the subject of a satirical skit performed by gay Māori cabaret artist Mika at the Edinburgh Festival in 1998. Mika claimed to have created the first indigenous queer chant. According to the *Australian*:

> In Edinburgh his queer take on the traditional Māori haka — the tongue waggling warriors chant familiar to viewers of rugby union — attracted plenty of interest and he is now booked internationally until November.[3]

Since then the flamboyant Mika has gone on to create a one-man entertainment enterprise ranging from his performances through to offering courses and workshops, and selling merchandise. He has also started a Mika museum!

Just two years later in 2000 Ngāti Rangiwewehi and Te Mātārae-i-o-Rehu combined to send 50 performers to the Edinburgh Tattoo. For the seasoned Edinburgh Tattoo observer the contrast between kapa haka and the traditional entertainments could not have been more dramatic.

Few would have expected that the key exhibit in attracting thousands of visitors to a Canadian exhibition stand at Telecom 99, in Geneva, would be a haka party. London-based haka group Ngāti Rānana was hired to perform for Canada's Newbridge

The one-man kapa haka: Mika Haka

Photographs Sarah Orme

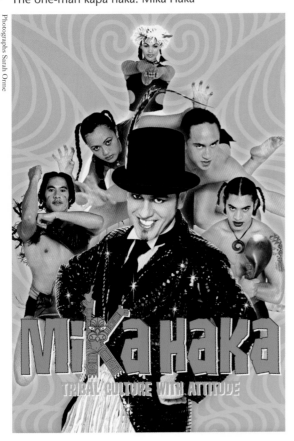

Network stand with hourly haka performances. The company was a sponsor for the Canadian Rugby Team which was playing at the 1999 Rugby World Cup.[4]

In the 1990s the haka was used as part of an industrial relations dispute between security guards and their bosses in Sydney. A group of security guards took exception to the lack of progress with their negotiations with the AMP insurance company over wages owed them for working at an AMP site. According to the *Dominion*:

> A 30-strong haka party arising from an industrial relations dispute stopped traffic on a downtown Sydney street for about 20 minutes . . . The men, helped by friends and colleagues, aired their grievances with a haka on Pitt St and then repeated the Maori challenge at AMP's headquarters nearby.[5]

These incidents indicate very clearly that the haka has become a novel form of national expression. It is also clear that young Aotearoa New Zealanders travelling overseas are becoming more adept at expressing themselves when they perform the haka. It certainly is an improvement on the mangled versions that young Aotearoa New Zealanders performed, often at pubs or parties, in the 1960s and 1970s.

There has been an upsurge in demand for haka groups to perform for functions in Aotearoa New Zealand and to support Aotearoa New Zealand trade delegations and other official functions overseas. This has seen the emergence of a group of younger entrepreneurial Māori establishing small, tightly disciplined groups of skilled entertainers ready to perform, subject to successful commercial negotiations.

In the past, this demand for smaller haka groups had usually been met through invitations being forwarded to the established national kapa haka groups or well-known regional groups for local events. Over recent times these groups have themselves established smaller teams to cater for the increasing domestic and international demands for their services.

The advent of the internet and the ready availability of information have widened the choice for those seeking haka groups to perform. A number of the major national and regional haka groups have established their own websites tailored to the commercial market.

At the forefront of converting kapa haka knowledge and skill into commercial advantage are Ngāpo (Bub) and Pimia (Nan) Wehi. Ngāpo and Nan have an enviable record of success at the national Te Matatini Festival, the pre-eminent forum for kapa

Turanga Wahine Turanga Tane perform the Jubilee Pōwhiri at the Gisborne Girls' High School 50th Jubilee in 2006.

haka performers. They are the only tutors in Aotearoa New Zealand to have won at these competitions five times. They won on three occasions with the Auckland group, Te Waka Huia, and twice with the Gisborne-based group Waihīrere.

In 1986 the Wehi whānau established Pounamu Ventures, a Māori performing arts company based in Auckland. The groups trained by Bub and Nan have performed at prestigious events in numerous overseas locations and here in Aotearoa New Zealand — including at US President Bill Clinton's visit.

Bub Wehi has very firm views about the role of haka as a medium for educating Māori:

It requires great discipline and it's character building. It's a way of attaching yourself to your roots and being content with yourself, your past, your present situation and your future.[6]

In 1989 Bub and Nan established another company called Pounamu Training Systems. Since 1995 they have become registered trainers with the New Zealand Qualifications Authority.

Other entrepreneurial Māori who have seen an opportunity to combine the best of Māori culture with tourism and with other forms of entertainment include Puka Moeau and his partner Pania Papa. They recently produced a stage production of the highly acclaimed movie *Whale Rider* and contracted Pounamu Ventures to provide the kapa haka performers.

Another nationally known figure has also branched into commercialising kapa haka events. Willie Te Aho has set up an annual kapa haka competition called 'Super 12', which is aimed at providing opportunities for kapa haka groups to express their creativity and the development of Māori culture into new spaces. The 12 teams in the competition are

Courtesy Te Waka Huia. Photographer Aaron Smale

Under Ngāpo (Bub) and Pimia (Nan) Wehi's guidance, Te Waka Huia won the Te Matatini kapa haka competition three times.

required to perform a similar range of items, as seen in the Te Matatini Festival, in a period of 12 minutes. Teams are given free reign to be innovative and challenging while acknowledging their ancestral heritage.

These are just some of the ways in which the profile of haka is changing and its use is being internationalised. It will continue to evolve in style and content, and in purpose and performers, as new generations of Māori and Pākehā Aotearoa New Zealanders proudly embrace the country's unique art form.

Haka — a national icon?

Over recent decades Aotearoa New Zealanders have become very much used to seeing and revelling in the use of the haka by our sporting teams. We thrill to the spectacle of an All Black rugby team lining up prior to kick-off, whether at Twickenham, Ellis Park, Stadium Australia or Stade de France.

In September 2007 we again observed the gathering of the rugby nations to combat in France, where the Rugby World Cup was held. The meticulous planning by coach Graham Henry and his coaching team, the personal growth and commitment by team members led by Richie McCaw and the addition of a thrilling new haka, 'Kapa o Pango', to their arsenal meant that the All Blacks were totally focused on performing well.

To a certain extent we have become somewhat blasé about the haka and assume that it has always been a part of our history, especially our sporting history. Few Aotearoa New Zealanders have stopped to consider the meaning of the haka or delve into its traditional significance and origins. Yet there is abundant evidence to suggest that the haka is having a growing influence on our lives.

Chris Laidlaw, former All Black, in his reaction to the complaint by the New Zealand Government about a whisky advertisement on Belgian TV, noted that:

> The haka, just like so many other ancient cultural practices, has greatly evolved over the last century and a half. It is no longer simply a Maori form of expression. It has been borrowed, adopted, adapted, abused and popularised. It has been absorbed into the wider Pakeha culture as a novel form of national expression and it is a distinctive way that [Aotearoa] New Zealanders can express themselves, not always with much expertise, in other parts of the world.[7]

Regardless of All Black wins or losses, the haka itself remains untarnished by its most public performers. The haka is bigger than rugby. It is an icon which most Aotearoa New Zealanders are proud to identify with.

As the population of Māori grows beyond one million by 2050, and the ethnic demography of our country changes from its dominant whiteness to a browner blend incorporating Māori, Polynesian and Asian Aotearoa New Zealanders, we will become much more rooted in the soil of Aotearoa. As this happens, it is hoped that Māori language and culture will be shared by more and more Aotearoa New Zealanders as something that will bind them together.

Our pathway forward will have been paved by a haka, 'Ka Mate!', composed in the early 1800s to meet a moment of great personal challenge. It has been carried forward into the twenty-first century as a means of defining who we are.

There are numerous haka besides 'Ka Mate!' that lie in our historical repositories or are

in current use among the tribes. These and other new haka will be performed as an integral part of our growing awareness that we all belong to Aotearoa New Zealand.

Given the penchant for Aotearoa New Zealanders to embrace the haka 'Ka Mate!' it is interesting to speculate on whether the new haka 'Kapa o Pango' will gain the same degree of notoriety and fame as Kiwis place their stamp on the many parts of the world we travel to.

Haka and cultural vigour

One of the primary drivers for the continued survival and re-energising of Māori culture has been the introduction of inter-tribal cultural competitions. In a sense these competitions within and between tribes have become the modern-day substitute for the more violent clashes of the past. Within a disciplined format and a controlled environment, Māori are now able to give free reign to their talents and skills. While many groups continue to perform traditional items, composers are increasingly developing new materials to meet the changing nature and circumstances of the society in which we live.

Writing in the late 1940s, Sir Peter Buck observed that:

The haka have . . . been carried on for social reasons because they still constitute the heartiest form of welcome which a receiving tribe can give its visitors on important occasions.[8]

Buck lamented the passing of the old skills, as haka seemed to be performed only for English royalty or their representatives in ceremonies which he thought had become harder to revive with each passing generation.

Buck attributed the decline in skills and competence to the onset of European education and culture. Māori children learned games and dances from their Pākehā schoolmates and abandoned those passed down from their ancestors:

The skill to quiver the fingers and the elasticity of the protruding tongue seem to decrease with the ratio of increase in European education and culture.[9]

Some 50 years on, Buck would be amazed at the transformation that has taken place in the schools and within broader Aotearoa New Zealand society. Far from dying out, Māori culture is alive and flourishing. Many children of all ethnicities learn action songs and haka at school. It is a tribute to the non-Māori teachers and the colleges of education that this upsurge of interest in Māori culture has taken place in our schools. Certainly, though, the renaissance in Māori culture and in particular the performing arts has not happened overnight.

A new generation

In finishing it is apposite for me to relate two recent events that have affected me personally, which give credence to the thesis about the enduring universality of the haka and the place of kapa haka in our lives.

As I began the task to review and update this book my daughter, Rakaitemania, had started at Wellington Girls' College. She chose this college in part because it had a kapa haka team as she has become passionate about kapa haka. Wellington Girls' College has combined with Wellington College, a boys' school, to train a joint team to enter the Wellington regional secondary schools kapa haka competition.

Already the combined team has held a number of weekend training sessions following a punishing schedule to get them ready for the competition. The intensity of preparation is plain to see.

Rakaitemania has her poi with her most of the time and she practises night and day. The level of skills has risen dramatically over the past decade and the secondary school kapa haka competitions truly mirror the senior Te Matatini Festival for dedication and discipline.

In my daytime job I am currently completing an assignment as the Chief Executive Officer of Te Whare Wānanga o Awanuiārangi. In early June 2007, a group of 19 Hawaiians from Windward Community College paid us a visit to learn about Māori culture and to experience the way in which we approached education, lived our lives and practised our culture.

As part of their stay with us the Hawaiians had to study te reo, and learn waiata and a haka. On the eve of their departure, after a two-week stay, the group performed their traditional dances for the staff and public of Whakatāne. Their surprise items were the poi and a haka. As the men of the group started with their haka you could sense the anticipation and excitement among the largely Māori audience.

Centuries ago in central Polynesia our respective ancestors had taken decisions on travel. The Hawaiians ended up in the Northern Pacific thousands of kilometres from central Polynesia. We ended up some 3000 kilometres in the opposite direction. And while we have been separated for a thousand years at opposite ends of the Pacific, on the night of their concert we were once again bonded.

It was a pleasure for us to see the ready facility with which our 'relations' adapted to our more aggressive style of performance. It was equally enlightening to see how they had evolved in their performance styles, which were a lot gentler than we are used to. Above all it demonstrated how cultural performances can strengthen relationships. It is a lesson that our fellow Aotearoa New Zealanders are slowly coming to grips with.

Glossary

Aotearoa	New Zealand (Land of the long white cloud)
haka peruperu	haka with weapons
haka taparahi	haka without weapons
hāngī	earth oven
hapū	sub-tribe
hongi	to press noses and share breath in greeting
hui	meeting, gathering
iwi	tribe
kaihoe	rowers, paddlers
kapa haka	group of 'dancers'
karakia	religious incantations
karanga	call of welcome
kaumātua	elder
kaupapa	cause, purpose
kīnaki	relish, complement
koromiko	a shrub
kūmara	sweet potato
Māori	indigenous people of Aotearoa New Zealand
mana	prestige
manuhiri	visitor(s)
mānuka	a shrub or small tree
marae	village or traditional gathering place
mauri	life force
mere	short fighting club
Ngāti Awa	iwi in the Eastern Bay of Plenty
Ngāti Pikiao	iwi of the Te Arawa confederation of tribes

Ngāti Porou	iwi of the East Coast of the North Island
Ngāti Raukawa	iwi of the Tainui Confederation of tribes
ope	party or group
pā	Māori village which could be fortified or unfortified
Pākehā	Aotearoa New Zealander of European ancestry
pōhiri/pōwhiri	welcome process
pūkana	enlarging the whites of the eyes
Rūaumoko	god of earthquakes and volcanoes
tangata whenua	host(s)
tangihanga	(often abbreviated to tangi) funeral ceremony
tauā	war party
tikanga	protocol
tohunga	spiritual advisor, expert
tuatara	a lizard-like reptile
Tūhoe	iwi of the Urewera known as 'the children of the mist'
Tūmatauenga	god of war
utu	revenge
waiata	song
wairua	spirit or essence
waka	canoe(s)
wero	ceremonial challenge to visitors
whakaara	prelude
whānau	family/extended family
wharenui	meeting house (often carved)
whātero/whētero	protrusion of the tongue
wiriwiri	shimmer

Endnotes

Introduction: Personal reflections

1 Armstrong, A and Ngata, R 1964, *Maori Action Songs*, AH & AW Reed, Wellington.

Chapter 1: Haka in legend

1 Grey, Sir G 1906, *Polynesian Mythology and Ancient Traditional History of the New Zealand Race*, George Routeledge & Sons, London, pp. 65–71.
2 Stafford, DM 1967, *Te Arawa*, Reed, Wellington, pp. 32–33.
3 Jones, P Te H 1995, *Nga Iwi o Tainui*, Auckland University Press, Auckland, pp. 145–49.
4 Ibid.

Chapter 2: Haka variations

1 Williams, HW 1985, *A Dictionary of the Maori Language*, Government Printer, Wellington.
2 Armstrong A 1964, *Maori Games and Hakas*, AH & AW Reed, Wellington, p. 3.
3 Andersen, JC 1934, *Maori Music with Its Polynesian Background*, Thomas Avery & Sons, New Plymouth, p. 307.
4 Buck, Sir P 1987, *The Coming of the Maori*, Maori Purposes Fund Board, Wellington, p. 243.
5 Armstrong, A, op. cit., p. 3.
6 McLean, M and Orbell, M 1990, *Traditional Songs of the Maori*, Auckland University Press, Auckland, p. 21.
7 Armstrong, A, op. cit., p. 120.
8 McLean, M 1996, *Maori Music*, Auckland University Press, Auckland, pp. 57–75.
9 Ibid.
10 Awatere, Lt Col A 1975, *The Journal of the Polynesian Society*, Dec., Vol. 84, no. 4, Wellington.
11 McLean, M, op. cit., pp. 47–57.
12 Armstrong, A, op. cit., p. 121.
13 *Te Ao Hou (The New World)*, No. 26, March 1959.

14 Best, E and Evans, J (eds) 2001, *Notes on the Art of War*, Reed, Auckland, pp. 178–79.
15 Ibid., pp. 175–82.
16 Ngata, Sir A (ed.) and Jones, P Te H (trans.) 1980, *Nga Moteatea Part 3*, The Polynesian Society, Wellington, Song No. 221, pp. 91–97.
17 McLean, M, op. cit., p. 57.
18 Ibid., p. 376.
19 Shennan, J 1984, *The Maori Action Song*, NZ Council for Educational Research, Wellington, p. 67.

Chapter 3: The tradition of haka

1 Salmond, A 1991, *Two Worlds*, Penguin Books, Auckland, pp. 80–81.
2 Ibid.
3 Ibid.
4 Ibid.
5 Ibid.
6 Ibid., p. 126.
7 Ibid., p. 146.
8 Ibid., pp. 80–81.
9 Shennan, J 1984, op. cit., p. 5.
10 Ibid.
11 Ibid.
12 Ibid.
13 Ibid., p. 9.
14 Salmond, A 1990, *Hui*, Heinemann Reed, Wellington, p. 115.
15 Shennan, J, op. cit., p. 9.
16 Best, E and Evans, J (eds) 2001, op. cit., pp. 175–78.
17 Ibid.

Chapter 4: 'Ka Mate!' — the most famous haka of all

1 Oliver, WH 1990, *Ngā Tāngata Taumata Rau 1769–1789*, Allen & Unwin, Wellington, pp. 296–303.

2 Grace, JH 1959, *Tūwharetoa*, AH & AW Reed, Wellington, pp. 260–64.

3 Stafford, DM 1967, *Te Arawa*, Reed, Wellington, pp. 175–80.

4 Ibid.

5 Ibid.

6 Jones, P Te H (trans.) 1959, *King Pōtatu*, The Polynesian Society, Wellington.

7 Grace, JH, op. cit., p. 262.

8 Ibid.

9 Evison, HC 1993, *Te Wai Pounamu*, Aoraki Press, Christchurch, pp. 53–56.

Chapter 5: Cultural resurgence through haka and kapa haka

1 Andersen, JC, op. cit., pp. 327–49.

2 Ibid.

3 Ibid.

4 Ramsden, E 1948, *Sir Apirana Ngata and Maori Culture*, AH and AW Reed, Wellington, pp. 14–16.

5 Sir Āpirana Ngāta sent Pine Tamahori to teach Ngāpuhi the haka 'Rūaumoko' to be performed for the welcoming of Governor-General Bledisloe at Waitangi in 1934.

6 Ramsden, E, opt. cit., p. 20

7 Royal Visit Programme (Nelson Park, Napier), 25 February 1986.

Chapter 6: Tribal haka composers

1 *Te Ao Hou*, No. 26, March 1959.

2 *Te Ao Hou*, Spring edition, 1954, p. 15.

3 Ibid.

Chapter 7: Women and haka

1 Mahuika, AT 1973, MA thesis (Massey University), *The Female Leaders of Ngati Porou*.

2 Bidwell, JC 1841, *Rambles in New Zealand*, WS Orr and Co., London, pp. 313–14.

3 Ibid.

4 Andersen, JC, op. cit., pp. 214–15.

5 Best, E 1976, *Games and Pastimes of the Maori*, Government Printer, Wellington, p. 100.

6 Kāretu, T 1993, *Haka — Dance of a Noble People*, Reed, Auckland, pp. 70–77.

7 Ibid.

8 Ibid., pp. 82–83.

9 Takurua, AK, 'Ngawai, Tuini Moetu Haangu, 1910–1965', *Dictionary of New Zealand Biography*, updated 7 April 2006, www.dnzb.govt.nz

10 Ka'ai, TM, 'Pewhairangi, Te Kumeroa Ngoingoi 1921–1985' *Dictionary of New Zealand Biography*, updated 7 April 2006, www.dnzb.govt.nz

Chapter 8: War and haka

1 Mitcalfe, B 1974, *Māori Poetry*, Price Milburn for Victoria University Press, Wellington, p. 178.

2 Condliffe, JB 1971, *Te Rangi Hiroa: The Life of Sir Peter Buck*, Whitcombe & Tombes, Christchurch, p. 132.

3 Ibid.

4 Gardiner, Wira 1992, *Te mura o te ahi: The story of the Maori Battalion*, Reed, Auckland.

5 Gullery, C 1998, Cover of 'Haka Premiere', *Army News*, 17 February.

6 Notes provided by Sergeant Major of the Army WO1 HC Collier, 22 July 2001.

7 Ashton, L 2001, 'Blazing a Trail', *Mana*, June–July, pp. 24–27.

8 Sutherland ILG 1949, *The Ngarimu Hui; VC Investiture Meeting 1943*, Polynesian Society, Wellington.

9 Ibid.

10 Mahuika, AT, op. cit.

Chapter 9: Kapa haka and Te Matatini

1 Te Matatini website, www.tematatini.org.nz

2 http://www.atmpas.org.nz/history/history1.htm

3 NZQA, June 2000, Issue 1, www.nzqa.govt.nz

4 Te Matatini website, op. cit.

5 Ibid.

Chapter 10: The All Blacks and 'Ka Mate!'

1 Internet interview by *The Times* newspaper.

2 Ibid.

3 Lewis, P, *New Zealand Listener*, December 16–22, Vol. 206, No. 3475.

4 Palenski, R 2001, *Sunday Star-Times*, 21 January, p. 5.

5 Green, H 2001, letter to editor, *Waikato Times*, 27 January, p. 6.

6 Rendell, S 2001, *Evening Post*, 15 January.
7 Berry, R 2000, *Evening Post*, 13 June, p. 3.
8 Editorial 2000, 'The Great Haka Debate', *Nelson Mail*, 18 June, p. 7.
9 *Te Karere* 2001, TV One, 26 June.
10 New Zealand Rugby Museum (Palmerston North): www.rugbymuseum.co.nz
11 Blog site: www.rugby-pioneers.com
12 Stokes, J, Sports Reporter, BBC Sport Website, 15 November 2001
13 Ibid.
14 Gilhooly, D, *New Zealand Herald*, Sunday 26 November, Cardiff.
15 Gray, W, *New Zealand Herald*, Sunday 26 November, Cardiff.
16 Cleary, M, *Daily Telegraph*, Sports Writer, blog site.

Chapter 11: The All Blacks' new haka — 'Kapa o Pango'

1 Stokes J, *New Zealand Herald*, 2 July 2006.
2 New Zealand Rugby Football Union Inc., Media Release: 'All Blacks Add New Haka', 27 August 2005.
3 Ibid.
4 Sportonline@your.abc.net.au
5 Stokes, J, *New Zealand Herald*, 29 July 2006.
6 Ibid.
7 Farrar, D, DPF's Kiwiblog, Posting 28 November 2005.
8 National Party Official Website – Super Blues.
9 Stokes, J, *New Zealand Herald*, 29 August 2005.

Chapter 12: Other sports and haka

1 Sports and Recreation Council, *Integrating Maori and Sporting Culture*, Press Release, 23 June 2004.
2 RunnersWeb.com website, 24 October 2004.
3 Wolff, A, Senior Sports Writer, *Sports Illustrated*, posted on website 31 August 2002, SI.com.

4 Brad Walter, *Sydney Morning Herald*, 21 October 2006.
5 Mason, W, Personal Column, *Australian Star*, 16 October 2006.
6 Brad Walter, *Sydney Morning Herald*, 21 October 2006

Chapter 13: Haka and politics

1 Haselhurst, KM 1988, *Racial Conflict and Resolution in New Zealand*, Peace Research Centre, Canberra, p. 7.
2 Ibid., p. 5.
3 Ibid., p. 48.
4 Ibid., p. 17.
5 Wikipedia, 'Tame Iti' entry, http://en.wikipedia.org/wiki/Tame_Iti
6 Aotearoa Independent Media Centre: www.indymedia.org.nz
7 www.aotearoa.wellington.net.nz

Chapter 14: Haka and bad taste

1 NZ Post Website; 2 June 2006; *Daily Post* (Rotorua), June–July 2006; www.scoop.co.nz/stories/BU0606/S00039.htm
2 BBC Website, 9 January 2007
3 Cath Bennett, *Sydney Morning Herald*, 8 January 2007

Chapter 15: Haka and the global village

1 Author unknown 2001, *Dominion*, 4 January, p. 4.
2 *Dominion*, 2001, 5 January, p. 3.
3 McLean, M 1998, *The Australian*, 23 January, p. 17.
4 Pamatatau, R 1999, *New Zealand Infotech Weekly*, 18 October, p. 25.
5 Author unknown 2000, *Dominion*, 18 August, p. 1.
6 NZQA, June 2001, Issue 01, www.nzqa.govt.nz
7 Laidlaw, C 2001, *The Press*, 26 January, p. 28.
8 Buck, Sir P, op. cit., p. 250.
9 Ibid.

Index